RAPID
RESPONSE
TEAMS

PROVEN STRATEGIES
FOR SUCCESSFUL IMPLEMENTATION

Della M. Lin, MD

Rapid Response Teams: Proven Strategies for Successful Implementation is published by HCPro, Inc.

Copyright 2005 HCPro, Inc.

HCPro, Inc. provides information resources for the healthcare industry. A selected listing of other HCPro newsletters and books is found in the back of this book.

HCPro, Inc. is not affiliated in any way with the Joint Commission on Accreditation of Healthcare Organizations.

Della M. Lin, MD, Author
Jay Kumar, Senior Managing Editor
Paul Amos, Group Publisher
Jean St. Pierre, Director of Operations
Laura Godinho, Cover Designer
Jackie Diehl Singer, Graphic Artist
Jerrie Hildebrand, Layout Artist
Suzanne Perney, Publisher

Advice given is general. Readers should consult professional counsel for specific legal, ethical, or clinical questions.

Arrangements can be made for quantity discounts.

HCPro, Inc.
P.O. Box 1168
Marblehead, MA 01945
Telephone: 800/650-6787 or 781/639-1872
Fax: 800/639-8511 or 781/639-2982
E-mail: *customerservice@hcpro.com*

Visit HCPro at its World Wide Web sites:

www.hcpro.com and *www.hcmarketplace.com*

CONTENTS

CONTENTS

About the Author

Della M. Lin, MD

Della M. Lin, MD, is a former inaugural Health Forums Patient Safety Leadership fellow—a joint collaboration between the American Hospital Association and the National Patient Safety Foundation (NPSF). She has been a speaker at the last two NPSF Annual Patient Safety Congresses and has also been a speaker for several HCPro, Inc., audioconferences relating to patient safety and is a member of the Estes Park (CO) Institute Faculty. Lin is a practicing anesthesiologist, and has served on the American Society of Anesthesiologists Patient Safety Committee. She is also the executive director of continuing medical education at the Queen's Medical Center, Honolulu. Lin has more than 15 years of physician leadership experience, having served as department chief of anesthesiology, on hospital medical executive committees (MEC), peer review and credentialing committees, and currently as a board member at various healthcare entities. She is a consultant, lecturer, and author. She also acts as a facilitator for organizations and hospitals for their MEC and credentialing committee retreats; external peer review activities; in integrating patient safety initiatives; for disruptive physician interventions, and in developing postgraduate education programs, multidisciplinary performance improvement programs, and physician leadership.

INTRODUCTION

The literature regarding rapid response teams makes a compelling argument about catching the warning signs of patients in distress. The question healthcare professionals must ask is also compelling: Are some hospital deaths predictable and preventable?

This possibility is humbling to those of us who pride ourselves in providing high-quality care. In hospital after hospital, a review of cases and systems reveals too many instances of gaps, missed signals, and failed coordination that result in serious patient complications and possibly deaths.

These findings make it clear that we must improve the way that we bring timely care to our patients.

Increased documentation of effectiveness

Over the past four years, a growing number of studies have been published in peer-reviewed journals regarding rapid response teams (RRT) (also called medical emergency teams (MET) and medical response teams (MRT)), which are being created throughout the world.

In Victoria, Australia, one such team led by Rinaldo Bellomo, MD, found that instituting a critical care–based medical emergency team (MET)—consisting of an intensive care unit (ICU) physician, ICU nurse, and respiratory therapist—decreased the number of cardiac arrests and postsurgical complications, as well as overall hospital mortality.[1, 2]

In the ***British Medical Journal***,[3, 4] Michael Buist, MBChB, FRACP, FJFICM, wrote that his Melbourne, Australia-based team at Dandenong Hospital found a 50% drop in unexpected cardiac arrests following MET implementation. In addition, the team's findings suggested that several predictable physiologic signs could be used to identify a patient in trouble.

In the United States, Michael DeVita, MD, of the University of Pittsburgh Medical Center found that a 17% decrease in cardiac arrests of was associated with a concomitant increase in the use of METs.[5]

Key findings

The aforementioned hospital studies contained the following key findings at participating facilities:

- Remarkable drops in their cardiac arrest numbers within months of implementation.
- Significant drops in the number of unanticipated ICU admissions
- Earlier rescue of patients resulting in improved survival rates and lower mortality rates

These findings are also associated with hospital cost savings due to fewer complications, fewer patient ICU days, and reduced lengths of stay.

For example, during an April 2005 HCPro audioconference, Bellomo estimated that his hospital had saved $28 million since it implemented the MET program in 2002.

Additionally, the studies confirm and support earlier studies that suggested that sudden, unanticipated (e.g., with no "do not resuscitate" order) in-hospital cardiac arrests are rare. Patients usually exhibit signs and symptoms of destabilization hours before they actually arrest.

Granted, on hindsight review of any case, it is much easier to "see" the destabilization. However, we still should ask whether our system of care is designed optimally to identify and rescue as many of these failing patients as possible. Can an RRT model help? Is it possible that in some ideal hospital world there would be no unanticipated cardiac or respiratory arrests in the non-ICU setting? Is it possible that one would never hear "Code Blue" on the floor?

Move into the spotlight

In December 2004, the Institute for Healthcare Improvement (IHI) recommended RRTs as part of its six-part campaign to encourage U.S. hospitals to save 100,000 lives by June 2006. The IHI calculated that this change alone could save an estimated 60,000 lives. Now that, as of August 2005 the campaign includes more than 2,600 hospitals, the drive to put RRTs in place in hospitals is even more vigorous.

In addition to the IHI, national magazines and newspapers (e.g., the July 18, 2005, *U.S. News and World Report*, and the December 1, 2004, Wall Street Journal) have reported on the potential benefit of implementing these teams in hospitals, thus raising the profile of RRTs and bringing public attention toward this intervention.

A study published in the June 2005 ***Lancet*** reported on a prospective study of 23 Australian hospitals. After baseline measurements over two months, 12 hospitals implemented an MET, and the other 11 did not change their programs. At first glance, the study demonstrated that there were no significant differences between the two groups. This apparent lack of difference provided a good opportunity to pause and reflect on success factors and replicability of RRT/MET programs in all hospitals.

On closer evaluation, however, the study included several notable points:

- Hospitals in both groups had an overall decrease in the number of cardiac arrests postimplementation. Were the context and attention given to METs in Australia such that all hospitals (including the controls) reflected MET-like implementation to some degree?

- A larger number of hospitals were needed to provide statistical power and sensitivity to the changes. The actual baseline data differed from the original baseline expectations used when creating the study design.

- Implementation within hospitals in the MET group was highly variable and not stringently controlled. For example, trigger criteria were not consistently applied.

- Some of the non-MET group hospitals, upon further inspection, had teams that functioned very much like METs.

These facts mean that such teams are not a simple drop-in module. The concept's implementation, initial success, and sustained success will require you to examine how it will fit within your hospital. You must

- determine your need
- define your team
- monitor and sustain your results
- consider the future

Creating an RRT will be just the start of redesigning and refining how you provide care as a team in the hospital.

This book is not meant to be a cookbook for your RRT; rather, it is meant to be a guide. It provides information and highlights questions and decision points that will be important for your organization to raise and resolve as you move toward successful implementation. Nearly a dozen organizations have generously shared their stories with us for use in this book. These facilities are anywhere from a few months to several years into their RRT implementation journey, and their case studies, referenced throughout the book, will provide you with lessons learned, tools, and templates to help you get your team up and running quickly and efficiently.

Endnotes

1. Bellomo R, Goldsmith D, Uchino S, et al. Prospective controlled trial of effect of medical emergency team on postoperative morbidity and mortality rates. *Crit Care Med.* 2004;32(4):916-921.

2. Bellomo R, Goldsmith D, Uchino S, et al. A prospective before-and-after trial of a medical emergency team. *Med J Aust.* 2003;179(6):283-287.

3. Buist MD, Moore GE, Bernard SA, Waxman BP, Anderson JN, Nguyen TV. Effects of a medical emergency team on reduction of incidence of and mortality from unexpected cardiac arrests in hospital: preliminary study. *BMJ.* 2002;324(7334):387-390.

4. Buist M, Bernard S, Nguyen TV, Moore G, Anderson J. Association between clinically abnormal observations and subsequent in-hospital mortality: a prospective study. *Resuscitation.* 2004;62(2):137-141.

5. DeVita MA, Braithwaite RS, Mahidhara R, Stuart S, Foraida M, Simmons RL. Use of medical emergency team responses to reduce hospital cardiopulmonary arrests. *Qual Saf health care.* 2004;13(4):251-254.

6. Hillman, K et. al. Introduction of the Medical Emergency Team (MET) system: a cluster-randomized controlled trial. *The Lancet.* 2005; 365:2091-9736.

CHAPTER ONE

DETERMINING THE NEED

<table>
<tr><td>

CHAPTER ONE

</td><td>

DETERMINING THE NEED

</td></tr>
</table>

Although the studies reviewed earlier support the implementation of RRTs, what about your hospital? This chapter examines how to determine the need for an RRT in your facility.

Assess the need in context of your own data

One of the most important tasks involves stepping back from the peer-reviewed literature and reviewing the baseline data from your own hospital. An easy, straightforward way to do so, as suggested by the IHI, is to examine the last 50 deaths that have occurred in your hospital and apply a 2x2 matrix *(www.ihi.org/NR/rdonlyres/CC13C05E-9435-4692-8D7B-771BBAF44C9C/2721/FinalMoveDot.pdf)*.

This matrix portrays on one axis whether the patient was an ICU admission, and on the opposing axis whether the patient was admitted for comfort care. The group of patients in the cross between a non-ICU/non-comfort care admission has been called box D or box #4. The patients that fall into this box are most likely to need rescue.

Decision point

Potentially one of the most critical decisions in starting your RRT is determining who owns the initiative.

Pause and reflect on who in the facility will drive this initiative and who will ultimately own it. Drivers may include members of the following groups:
- Hospital performance improvement
- Medical executive committee
- Risk management
- ICU team
- Code team
- Nursing management
- Patient safety committee

However, also consider how the hospital will prioritize this initiative. Will it be part of an overall quality plan? Will board members be able to articulate your aim for this initiative? Who will be your executive leadership sponsor? What will his or her role be? These issues may affect the program's sustainability.

Seven tips for success

1. Review your own numbers—you don't know what you don't know

- If you don't look, you won't know. After reviewing your own mortality data through the 2x2 matrix, another more focused review might include a review of your most recent 20–25 non-ICU codes (see Queens Medical Center case study). Doing so will help determine whether there is still an opportunity for improvement in the context of the systems that you have in place. Were there signs and symptoms six, 12, or 24 hours preceding the code? Was the physician contacted? Was there difficulty in reaching the physician? What triggers would have been initiated if a rapid response criteria system was used?

This review also will undoubtedly provide the team with case studies that help define the need. Other internal stories can help you define your need. Whether it be a new nursing graduate or a seasoned nurse, stories of frustration resulting from unclear communication about the coordination/planning or recognition of a deteriorating patient will provide insight into where you want to focus your RRT's initial interventions.

2. Provide a quick business case

Here are three quick ways to make a case to administration for RRT:

- It is much less costly and chaotic to have a team of two or three at the bedside, rather than a full code team of 10–15. The resources expended during a code event are tremendous. Simply reducing the number of codes will cut those expenses.

- Reducing the number of days of ICU stay lowers costs. The ICU is one of the more expensive areas in which to keep a patient. Avoiding those ICU transfers and reducing the number of days ultimately is a better use of resources.

- It can help decrease staff turnover. An unexpected but welcomed outcome in many hospitals that have implemented RRTs has been improved job satisfaction and better staff retention.

The cost of recruiting and orienting a new staff member is significant—above and beyond the staffing stress. Improved staff retention translates into hospital savings.

3. Check overall safety culture readiness

An RRT will face great challenges if the safety culture within the organization is not ready. A culture that upholds traditional hierarchy, creates barriers to speaking up, limited trust, overrides production goals, and expects strict policy adherence and perfection is likely the wrong culture in which to implement an RRT. Instead, check to see whether your organization and leadership walks the walk and puts safety as its top priority by reinforcing the following seven safe habits:

- Accept vulnerability
- Emphasize learning over judgment
- Be wary of assumptions
- Encourage constant communication
- Balance production and protection goals
- Value trust and transparency
- Establish hospital/performance and accountability goals related to safety

Strive toward the following characteristics of a high-reliability organization (Weick and Sutcliffe, Managing the Unexpected, 2001):

- Preoccupation with failure
- Reluctance to simplify interpretations
- Sensitivity to operations
- Commitment to resilience
- Deference to expertise

Kaiser Permanente's Northern California region has mandated that its staff receive human factors education and training in the communication technique SBAR (situation, background, assessment, recommendation/response). As Kaiser rolls out its RRTs, having this safety education as a backdrop is crucial to the success of the teams (see Kaiser case study).

4. Review other rescue systems already in place

There are undoubtedly certain rescue systems already in place in your hospital—one being the code team. You also may have stroke code teams or crisis nurses that are pulled into the care of a patient under certain circumstances. Smaller hospitals may use their emergency department (ED) staff or a nursing supervisor in some rescue roles.

Your RRT will function as an adjunct or as an evolution of these current existing systems. An overall review of these systems will allow for a more complete design and plan for the team.

5. Bring in stakeholders of your other rescue systems

The stakeholders of your other rescue systems may, in fact, be the core of your review and implementation team. These other rescue teams may be so overtaxed for their resources that an RRT will be a welcome addition. They also will be aware of front-line cases where missed opportunities for rescue may have occurred.

Alternatively, these rescue teams may feel threatened by the addition of an RRT. The idea that we are "failing to rescue" may be misinterpreted as a reflection of their competence. RRTs may seem to be a "flavor of the month" instead of a true care redesign. Therefore, the overall goals and desired improvements should be established and agreed upon.

6. Get support from your medical executive committee

Regardless of whether you decide on a physician-driven team, obtain support from the medical executive committee (MEC). Most hospital boards designate the MEC to oversee quality in the hospital. This initiative is too important to let it pass as an operational project, and it requires the endorsement and advocacy of your medical staff leadership.

7. Build from ground up and leadership down

Ideally, RRTs will have champions at various levels within the organization. The more levels, the more momentum. At the Queen's Medical Center in Honolulu, strong champions to build momentum came from a floor nurse and an ICU nurse who had advanced patient safety education (see case study), as well as a medical director, physicians on the MEC, and the chief nursing officer as the executive sponsor.

CHAPTER TWO

DEFINING AND SELECTING YOUR TEAM

CHAPTER TWO

DEFINING AND SELECTING YOUR TEAM

Many of our case study hospitals have identified defining and selecting your team as the most critical success factor for their RRTs.

Is there a definite "best practice" team model? The answer is a decided no. Hospitals have successfully implemented teams with many models, including the following combinations of members:

- Intensivist, ICU nurse, respiratory therapist

- Hospitalist, ICU nurse, respiratory therapist

- Two ICU nurses

- Physician assistant, ICU nurse, respiratory therapist

- Hospitalist, respiratory therapist

There are no absolutes as to which professional roles must be present. Teams have been successful without a respiratory therapist, without an ICU nurse, and without an ICU physician—or any physician.

Decision points

That having been said, resolve the following questions when defining and selecting your team:

1) Will this team be physician-driven or nurse-driven?

Because there is no perfect answer for this, consider the following to help you make this decision in the context of your organization:

- Define what interventions most need to be implemented by the RRT.

  For example, if you find that line placement is a common intervention and need in your rescue calls, then having a physician on the team would be appropriate.

  If you decide on a non-physician team, articulate what interventions the team can implement prior to receiving a physician order. These interventions should be codified by standing policy, approved by the medical staff (e.g., via the Medical Executive Committee).

  Examples of standing interventions can include:
  - Initiation of venous access
  - Ordering laboratory tests (e.g. H&H, ABG), diagnostic tests (e.g., CXR)
  - Administering vasocactive and antirhythmic drugs
  - Initiation of standing respiratory care protocols

See p. 20 for examples of some explicit protocols to consider

- Who is passionate about this initiative?

  If there is a physician who is enthusiastic about and committed to implementation and being part of the team, then having a physician-driven team may make sense. Similarly, if you have a choice of ICU nurses (e.g., medical versus surgical), choose your pilot teams based on a driven desire to see this program succeed.

- Don't go head on against resistance during your pilot phase.

  If there is great concern about taking nurses away from the ICU, then an RRT model that doesn't include an ICU nurse may fit your organization. However, keep in mind the unanticipated positive impact RRTs have had on ICU–floor nurse relationships in most hospitals that have included an RN on the team.

  Similarly, if there is significant push-back from attending physicians or if your physician resources are stretched, focusing on a nurse-driven team at the outset may be more prudent.

- You can change and be flexible about the team.

  The availability of resources may make it more practical to have an MD-driven team active during the day and a nurse-driven team at night. Again, there is no recipe for the teams that have been successful. There is no magic number and there are no absolutes in terms of individual members of the team. What has been far more important is articulating the role of the team as a unit and articulating the goal of the initiative.

2) Will team members also have regular patient care assignments?

Ideally, it would seem that team members should be free of specific patient care assignments. However, in actuality, most hospitals interviewed found that they had to use team members who also carried patient care responsibilities. If your hospital must do so, make sure it is clear how RRT members' patients will be covered while the individual is away. It is critically important to articulate and plan this coverage ahead of time. Brief the backup person about the patients at the outset of the shift, and keep him or her apprised of significant changes. When an RRT call comes in, time should not be wasted with patient care hand-off—at the same time, however, don't compromise the care of patients on the home unit.

Some organizations start with a team made of people with patient assignments but later move to a designated team. They have been able to present a business model for additional funding (see Hoag case study) after successful pilots and outcome results. Certainly, one can argue that the resources it takes to have 10–15 people present at a code compared to the two- or three-person RRT is worth the expenditure for dedicated staff.

Keep in mind that, in general, hospitals find average call rates to be about 10 calls/month/100 beds (15–25 calls/1,000 admissions). However, at the high end, hospitals have reported as many as 35+calls/month/100 beds (see North Carolina Baptist Hospital case study).

Tips for success

Consider the following when defining and selecting an RRT:

- **Select team members with good interpersonal skills**
  Communication skills and a desire to teach are crucial to the RRT roles. At North Carolina Baptist, the nurses on the team have significant educational roles that they carry out when their RRT calls are light.

- **Explicitly define roles and responsibilities**

  Doing so can clarify confusion as to the difference between a code call and an RRT call.
  Such roles and responsibilities might be defined as follows:

  - The team will respond to calls within five minutes
  - The team will collaborate with the primary patient care team to provide support and education
  - The team will assess the patient and, together with the primary nurse, communicate this assessment to the patient's attending physician
  - The team will initiate protocols as defined
  - The team will document calls in the RRT log record
  - The team will provide follow-up to the primary nurse/nursing unit within 12 hours of initial call

- **Consider a job description**

  A job description can outline not only the roles and responsibilities but also the clinical and
  collaborative skills of the RRT. For example, at Mercy Memorial Hospital in Des Moines (see
  case study), the RRT job description says that members must

  - have experience as a clinical nurse educator
  - have mentoring skills
  - have five years' ICU experience
  - demonstrate collaboration with another department

- **Expand the definition of the RRT role**

  Don't confine your decision of the RRT role to whether the individual will have patient care
  assignments. At Kaiser Sunnyside, the RRT nurse is supported at 0.5 full-time equivalent in
  the role of performance improvement data/outcome monitoring (see case study). At North
  Carolina Baptist, the RRT nurse is a "roving nurse." Not only is education a key part of the
  role, but these teams respond to calls initiated by physicians—not just for failing patients,
  but for patients the physician has not gotten around to visiting during rounds or who the
  physician might identify as benefiting from a more frequent assessment (see case study).

- **Train RRT members as a team**

  The team dynamics of the RRT are be important for successful application. A three-member
  team that includes an ICU nurse, ICU physician, and supervisory RT is made of traditionally
  autonomous individuals. Therefore, help team members learn to work together by training

them in

- situational awareness

- briefings

- anticipating and communicating planned and possible events

- cross-checking and verifying

- providing follow-up

Tools such as role-playing scenarios and SBAR (a communication tool known as Situation, Background, Assessment, Recommendation/Response; see sidebar for more information) have been very effective in training many RRTs. Simulation is also an excellent training method for RRTs (see sidebar). In particular, coaching the team on the barriers created by professional and cultural hierarchy—and their role in breaking down those barriers—will facilitate the positive effect of earlier calls to the RRT.

- **Consider formal training**

Some organizations (see Jewish Hospital case study) use external formal clinical skills training. The Society for Critical Care Medicine provides a course entitled Fundamentals in Critical Care Support (*www.sccm.org/education/fccs_courses/index.asp*).

The framework for the two-day course is as follows:

Course purpose:

- To better prepare the non-intensivist for the first 24 hours of management of the critically ill and injured patient until transfer or appropriate critical care consultation can be arranged

- To assist the non-intensivist in dealing with sudden deterioration of the critically ill and injured patient

- To prepare house staff for ICU coverage

- To prepare nurses and other critical care practitioners to deal with acute deterioration in the critically ill and injured patient

Course objectives:

- Prioritize assessment needs for the critically ill and injured patient

- Select appropriate diagnostic tests

- Identify and respond to significant changes in the unstable patient

- Recognize and initiate management of acute life-threatening conditions

- Determine the need for expert consultation/patient transfer and prepare the practitioner for optimally accomplishing transfer

However you define your team, review the resources and rescue systems you currently have in place within your hospital. Once you have defined what your team might look like, make sure to select the team members not just for clinical skills but for communication skills as well. As is often said in the human resources corporate world, "Don't hire for skill, hire for attitude."

FIGURE
2.1

WHAT IS SBAR?

Communication is the most frequently cited causal factor in sentinel events. All too often, in the midst of a clinical situation, a conversation between two individuals results in miscommunication, lack of communication, or lack of focus in the communication. Any of these disconnects can result in breakdowns ranging from a slight delay in resolving to a problem to a catastrophic outcome.

SBAR is a mnemonic device that has received increased attention within the healthcare industry in recent years. This communication tool originates from the U.S. Navy nuclear submarine industry. Doug Bonacum, vice president of patient safety at Kaiser Permanente of Colorado and a former lieutenant commander on nuclear submarines, was the first to make the link to healthcare. Simply, the mnemonic stands for the following:

S: Situation

B: Background

A: Assessment

R: Recommendation/response

For example, in a RRT call, the floor nurse might relay the following using the SBAR method:

S: Mr. Jones is a patient with a significant change in his respiratory status. He has gone from requiring 2-L NP O2 to a 7L mask to maintain his oxygen saturation at 92%.

B: He is two days s/p a total knee replacement, receiving a PCA for pain management, his pulse rate is in the 80s, and his last BP was 110/70.

A: I think he may need a respiratory treatment or some type of respiratory support.

R: I'd like the RRT to see him for additional assessment.

FIGURE
2.1

WHAT IS SBAR? (CONT.)

Like the SOAP (subjective, objective, assessment, plan) mnemonic that many in healthcare use for standardizing progress notes, SBAR as a communication tool attempts to standardize the way we communicate in clinical situations.

When used effectively during RRT calls, the SBAR communication tool provides a way to plan all four parts of the communication **before** communicating. The tool often allows one to reflect on the intent of the call and to clear out extraneous information that may only distract and cause the conversation to lose focus. It forces one to ask, "Why am I really calling this individual, and what is it I want from him or her?"

Many factors can influence the way we approach an individual for a conversation. For example, if we historically have had uncomfortable and unsuccessful conversations with an individual, we are likely to avoid such confrontations as much as possible. In healthcare, it is apparent that professional hierarchy, gender, ethnic differences, and organizational culture all influence open communication. Even the way we individually organize data and arrive at diagnoses and plans can vary between specialties. Some are more thorough and detail-oriented, and others approach data in a larger framework, with quick pattern-recognition.

Furthermore, even such factors as the time of day may influence whether an individual will call in a concern and how he or she may frame it. For example, a gut feeling of "something going wrong" with a patient may not be reported as quickly at 3 a.m., when it may disturb a physician at home, compared to at 9 a.m. Similarly, a floor team that knows a surgeon is in the operating room at 8 a.m. may wait until after the scheduled surgery to contact the surgeon about a "nagging feeling" regarding a patient's condition.

SBAR is a quick, concise methodology that removes many of the barriers to communication and allows for a clear presentation of the information.

In general, the nursing medical profession tends to present information in a narrative, descriptive, and holistic manner—i.e., the situation and the background. In comparison, physicians tend to focus on problem solving and therefore direct their attention toward the assessment and the recommendation/response. By understanding these professional differences in communication style, SBAR can be used to move the conversation through all four important bullet points, resulting in concise information relevant to a decision being passed along effectively.

FIGURE
2.1

WHAT IS SBAR? (cont.)

Note, however, that SBAR is not just a nursing/physician communication tool. You can use it to lower barriers and improve communication between seasoned nurses and new nurses, between ICU nurses and floor nurses, between technician staff and nurses, between office staff and patients, and between physicians of different specialties.

In the aforementioned case, after the RRT has evaluated the patient, a call might be made to the attending physician, as follows, using SBAR:

S: We wanted to update you on a change in Mr. Jones' condition. He had a significant change in his respiratory status and was evaluated by the rapid response team, which initiated a respiratory protocol with an albuterol nebulizer updraft treatment.

B: Mr. Jones' respiratory rate had gone up to 28, and he needed 7L mask O2 to maintain his O2 SATs at 92%. After receiving the respiratory treatment, he is more comfortable and we have him back on 3L O2 NP. His other vital signs have been essentially unchanged.

A: The respiratory treatment has made him comfortable for now.

R: We would like an order to continue treatments every two hours, while he is awake, for 24 hours. Would you also like a CXR to be ordered now or in the morning?

SBAR is being used by many RRTs as an integral communication model, both when the floor nurse calls the team and when the floor nurse or RRT calls the attending physician. In both sets of circumstances, the resulting clear and concise communication has received much positive feedback.

FIGURE
2.2

USING SIMULATION FOR TRAINING

Simulation is a powerful education tool, but it is particularly useful when starting and sustaining RRTs within a hospital: It provides the unique ability to re-create clinical scenarios in a safe environment, without putting patients at risk.

The Institute of Medicine's 1999 report *To Err is Human* supports the use of "simulations, whenever possible" to improve patient safety and the quality of healthcare delivery. The report adds that "crew resource management techniques, combined with simulation, have substantially improved aviation safety and can be modified for health-care use . . . Healthcare organizations should establish team training programs for personnel in critical care areas using proven methods . . . employed in aviation, including simulation."

The importance of simulation in RRT training is multifaceted. First, as an engaging educational tool, it gives a new initiative a higher profile. Second, it offers the ability to build and test the RRT implementation. For example, when conducting a simulated scenario, the staff and team can debrief and clarify the following:

- When to call
- What to say when calling
- How a team might respond
- What resources are available
- What challenges there might be in assessment and treatment

Have the team simulate potential complications and failures of care and "play out" various solutions. Compare and review the solutions, allowing the team to rehearse the best-case scenario.

Even the decision of whether the team should carry equipment (e.g., IV supplies, ABG supplies, Doppler blood pressure monitor, portable pulse oximeter monitor) might best be made through simulation of cases on various floors to determine the accessibility of the necessary equipment.

Third, the team will build important skills in decision-making, prioritization, and resource management, all of which are key to the true functioning of a team in a complex environment.

Finally, continue using simulation as ongoing education to reinforce case story learning and to develop educational skills and competency in clinical areas revealed through the review of rapid response call triggers. For example,

FIGURE

2.2

USING SIMULATION FOR TRAINING

if the recognition of acute renal failure and pulmonary edema are clinical scenarios where staff could benefit from clinical education and differential diagnosis. Simulation through case scenarios can reinforce the educational learning.

For all of these reasons, as you launch your RRT, consider simulation and situational rehearsal—whether by case scenario discussions or low-fidelity simulator mannequins—as an effective way to engage staff in active learning while teaching important concepts in both clinical and team skills.

EMERGENCY PROTOCOLS FOR NON-PHYSICIAN RRTs

The following emergency protocols may be initiated by the appropriate nursing staff (e.g., RRT) prior to receiving an order by a physician:

1. Respiratory Distress
   a. Non-intubated patient
   b. Intubated patient
2. Symptomatic hypotension
3. Chest pain
4. Symptomatic bradycardia
5. Sustained ventricular tachycardia
   a Hemodynamically stable
   b. Hemodynamically unstable
6. Pulseless ventricular tachycardia, ventricular fibrillation
7. Major hemorrhage
8. Acute altered mental status/unresponsiveness
9. Acute stroke

Examples of emergency protocols:

EMERGENCY PROTOCOLS
1. RESPIRATORY DISTRESS
1.1 NON-INTUBATED PATIENT
   a. Position patient to open airway
   b. Administer supplemental O2
   c. Apply continuous pulse oximetry
   d. Adjust O2 to keep O2 sat >92%
   e. Obtain ISTAT ABG
   f. Obtain Stat Portable Chest X-ray
   g. Suction as indicated
   h. Establish or verify patent large bore IV access
   i. If condition continues to deteriorate, use mask bag ventilation with 100% FI O2

Initiate Cardiopulmonary Resuscitation as indicated

Implement AHA Guidelines for ACLS as clinically indicated

Activate Code 500 System

Document clinical assessment and interventions

2. SYMPTOMATIC HYPOTENSION

2.1 Lie patient flat elevate lower extremities

2.2 Administer supplemental O2

2.3 Apply continuous pulse oximetry

2.4 Adjust O2 to keep oxygen saturation >92%

2.5 Establish or verify large bore IV access

2.6 Search for and treat reversible underlying cause

    Pulmonary Edema

    Volume Problem (shock)

    Pump Problem (MI)

Rate Problem (Bradycardia / Tachycardia)

2.7 Rapid bolus infusion of 500cc Normal Saline (in < 30 min)

Use caution patients with cardiac history of poor ventricular function

2.8 Initiate Dopamine Drip titrate to keep SBP > 90mmhg

2.9 If patient becomes tachycardic: wean dopamine

2.10 Initiate Levophed Drip titrate to keep SBP >90mmhg

    If patient continues to deteriorate,

    Initiate Cardiopulmonary Resuscitation as indicated

    Implement AHA Guidelines for ACLS as clinically indicated

    Activate Code Blue System as needed

    Document clinical assessment and interventions

3. CHEST PAIN

3.1 Administer supplemental O2

3.2 Apply continuous pulse oximetry

33 Adjust O2 to keep oxygen saturation >92%

3.4 Obtain stat 12 lead ECG

3.5 Give NTG 1/150 tablet S/L if SBP >100 mmgh

May repeat x2 if SBP >100mmhg

3.6 Establish or verify patent large bore IV access

3.7 Consider aspirin therapy

    Initiate Cardiopulmonary Resuscitation as indicated

    Implement AHA Guidelines for ACLS as clinically indicated

    Activate Code Blue System

    Document clinical assessment and interventions

4. SYMPTOMATIC BRADYCARDIA

Indicated by heart rate < 60 beats / minute with: Symptomatic Hypotension

4.1 Administer supplemental O2

4.2 Apply continuous pulse oximetry

4.3 Adjust O2 to keep oxygen saturation >92%

4.4 Establish or verify patent large bore IV access

5.5 Administer

    Atropine 0.5-1 mg IV push every 3-5 minutes

    Up to a total dose of 3 mg or 0.04 mg/kg

    Prepare for transcutaneous pacing

    If patient continues to deteriorate

    Initiate Cardiopulmonary Resuscitation as indicated

    Implement AHA Guidelines for ACLS as clinically indicated

    Activate Code 500 System

    Document clinical assessment and interventions

5. SUSTAINED VENTRICULAR TACHYCARDIA

HEMODYNAMICALLY STABLE

5.1 Administer supplemental O2

5.2 Apply continuous pulse oximetry

5.3 Adjust O2 to keep oxygen saturation >92%

5.4 Establish or verify patent large bore IV access

5.5 Administer

Amiodarone 150 mg in 100 cc D5W over 10 minutes

OR

Lidocaine 1-1.5 mg/kg IV push

If patient continues to deteriorate

Activate Code 500 System

Initiate Cardiopulmonary Resuscitation as indicated

Implement AHA Guidelines for ACLS as clinically indicated

Document clinical assessment and interventions

Source: Queen's Medical Center, Honolulu

CHAPTER THREE

IMPLEMENTATION CAVEATS

IMPLEMENTATION CAVEATS

Perhaps you have already defined and trained your team. Perhaps you have even trialed the system on a small pilot scale. What can we learn from hospitals that have been at this anywhere from three months to more than three years? What are important caveats to consider in your implementation strategy?

Decision points

Consider the following key decision points within the context of your organization:

Do we call the MD at the same time that we make the rapid response team (RRT) call, or do we call the MD after RRT assessment?

There are advantages to both decisions.

- Calling the attending physician at the same time as making the RRT call will do the following:

  o Reduce time and therefore any potential delays in reaching the physician. If your paging system may sometimes require an hour before the attending physician responds, an early call may be the correct strategy.

  o Reduce physician resistance. If you anticipate physician resistance in the form of perceived "being kept out of the loop" or taking control of patients, it may help to articulate clearly that a simultaneous call will go out to the physician.

- Waiting to make the call to the attending physician includes the following benefits:
  o Clear and more concise communication, with the added benefit of a second assessment. This is the comment we frequently hear from all parties—the attending physician, the floor nurse, and the RRT. After the RRT assessment, some hospitals will encourage the primary nurse to call the attending physician. The SBAR format is used to standardize the communication. (See SBAR figure).

o If the RRT is able to institute certain interventions—e.g., fluid bolus, respiratory treatment—these interventions will already be underway at the time of the call to the attending physician, which eliminates one step and the need to get permission for such interventions from a physician.

Should the team carry equipment to the call?

In the organizations that we interviewed, teams bring varying amounts of equipment to calls, including no equipment, a small tackle box, a small duffel bag, or a small, soft-sided, carry-on bag. All organizations felt their decisions were appropriate and had no plans to change them. The decision may come, in part, from the answers to two questions within the context of your organization:

o How standardized and accessible is your emergency equipment? If every unit has items (e.g., code cart, IV supplies, respiratory care adjuncts) in a standardized place, duffel bags are less critical. Have the teams visit the units and see whether they can, locate critical items themselves, when necessary. Simulate calls to help you make this determination (see Simulation sidebar).

o What interventions will the team carry out? The more types of interventions (e.g., noninvasive respiratory support, line insertions), the more likely that the team will have to carry some equipment. Some examples include
- intubation equipment
- IV equipment
- doppler blood pressure equipment
- pediatric lab tubes
- arterial blood gases kit
- pulse oximeter
- nebulizer equipment

Hospitals that have included drugs within these kits have them locked, packaged, and issued by the pharmacy to comply with medication management standards.

How to call

Will calls be initiated by pager/cell phone? Will the call go to one member or to all members of the team?

o If your organization focuses on a minimal response time for the RRT (e.g., less than two minutes, as with Missouri Baptist in St. Louis), a simultaneous page makes the most sense.

o Organizations caution against using an overhead page. Although it might seem intuitive to use an overhead page to ensure a faster response, hospitals have found that doing so makes people more hesitant to make the call—just as they are to activate the "Code Blue" call.

o Use an easy-to-remember number for the call. Hospitals have shared with us such call numbers as
- 777
- 411
- 911
- 4321
- 1234

Should we pilot this initiative or just roll out an RRT facilitywide?

Our case study experts have recommended both strategies (see Jewish Hospital and Missouri Baptist case studies). Your decision may depend on several factors:

o The readiness of your organization. With the increase in attention on RRTs, your hospital may be primed for a hospitalwide start.

o Size and complexity of your hospital.

o Whether you will have a fully designated RRT or one composed of members with other patient care duties. The capacity of the RRT to answer calls and ability to have back up for multiple calls may drive this decision.

o The ability of your organization to make and communicate changes easily. Whenever these initiatives get launched, early feedback results in nuances and modifications to the initial rollout plan. If your organization accepts these risks and can communicate the modifications easily, small pilot trials may not be as essential.

Should you decide to pilot your initiative, selecting a pilot unit can be important as well. You may wish to choose a unit that

- o has a demonstrated champion for the RRT.
- o may be identified as being able to use the RRT often. Pilot units often include units with
    - a high percentage of new nursing graduates
    - frequent codes
    - a high percentage of oncology patients
    - a high percentage of renal failure patients
    - a demonstrated interest in performance improvement change projects and learning from these projects

Should we focus on all units or specifically on the surgical floors?

The early RRT work from Australia focused particularly on postsurgical patients. Although most hospitals in the United States have not limited RRTs to surgical patients, review of outcomes specific to postsurgical complications and postsurgical reductions in length of stay have supported a definite benefit of such RRT interventions for the surgical patient.

Should we use specific criteria for calling the RRT?

The use of specific criteria appears to run a full circle, depending upon how far along you are in implementation.

Phase A: The start/pre-implementation:

Most hospitals initially include a vital-sign parameter list of criteria, similar to the following:

- o Change in respiratory status
    - RR<10
    - RR>28
    - O2 Sat < 90% despite O2 supplementation
- o Change in heart rate
    - HR<45
    - HR>125
- o Change in LOC from baseline
    - Confused, lethargic, agitated, unresponsive
- o Change in BP
    - SBP<90

o Change in urine output

- UOP<50cc/4 hours

o New or recurring chest pain

o Staff's gut feeling: "I'm worried," "something's wrong"

Phase B: Some hospitals place the staff's "gut feeling" at the top of the list. Others deleted the vital sign parameters altogether. Their rationale is that they want first and foremost to encourage the staff to call on a "gut feeling" and that placing rigid criteria may actually create a barrier to calling.

If the vital-sign parameters are deleted altogether as a criteria to initiate a call, the performance improvement arm in these hospitals often keeps these criteria on a post-call record to track the physiologic changes that have occurred. This information is then used for quality improvement opportunities.

Phase C: Later implementation phases

Hospitals are coming full circle and realizing that after the barriers to call are lowered and their programs have had some track record, cases are still being missed because criteria are not being used. These hospitals are now reinstituting the vital-sign parameters—sometimes within early warning systems (see chapter 5).

Ten tips for success

1. Respond! No questions asked

This tip is important—it ensures that the floor units will embrace the concept of the RRT. There should be no second-guessing of whether it was right or wrong to call the RRT, or whether the call came too early or too late.

2. Use an algorithm to clarify the process

A diagram of what happens once a call is activated—including how and when the attending physician is called and how continued care of the patient occurs in the event of a transfer to a higher level of care—will help explicitly outline the new process.

3. Tie in implementation with education of chain of command process and policy

Often, frontline staff are unclear about what the chain of command is within the hospital and how to activate it. If a physician cannot be reached and there is a significant patient care concern, does a call go to the department chief or vice president of medical affairs to handle the call? Since your RRT is part of a larger effort to avoid delays in care, staff should be able to articulate what escalation of calls need to occur from both a nursing and physician chain of command.

4. Consider using an acronym

Acronyms are a great way to foster awareness to a new initiative. At Integris Health, the pre-RRT program is named DUCS (Discovering Underlying Clinical Systems; see case study). At Southwestern Vermont, its SBAR tool is called SNAP (see case study).

5. Use stories and SBAR to educate the floor

Storytelling is a key ingredient to all patient safety initiatives, and implementation of your RRT is no exception. Ideally, these stories should come from your own institution, as buy-in is greatest when the story told is alive in your own backyard. It is not difficult to morph stories to avoid revealing specific names. However, as such cases are often rescues, changing staff identities does not appear to be as necessary (see Southwestern case study and the accompanying RRT story). Rolling out a common communication tool such as SBAR has been an important success factor for many hospitals. Integrating such standardized communication tools—verbally, in the medical record, and in the RRT call record—has focused RRT strategies into a focused call with quick intervention.

6. Use forcing function application to spread the word

Forcing function constraints help to drive or control behavior without relying on memory. A classic patient safety forcing function was the removal of potassium chloride at the bedside. It removed the need to remember the potential high-risk adverse events that can happen with potassium chloride and the need to dilute concentrated potassium chloride prior to administration.

Forcing function also constrains the user from doing one thing until another is done. For example, sliding the lever in the airplane bathroom constrains the user from turning on the light until the door is locked.

For RRTs, the following forcing functions help spread the word:

- Automatic response by rapid response team when a "respiratory STAT" call is made

- Automatic call to laboratory and imaging so they can be on alert and aware that an RRT call is made; it also recognizes a common need for diagnostic labs and chest X-ray to be done as a result of the RRT assessment

- Automatic follow-up to the floor after six hours when an RRT call has not resulted in a transfer to a higher level of care
- Automatic visit to the floor within 12 hours of a patient transfer from the ICU to the floor

- Automatic visit by the ICU nurse from the RRT to all floors with the question, "Who is your sickest patient today?"

7. Ensure that the floor nurse making the call stays with the patient

This is a critical factor in differentiating the RRT concept from the traditional "code blue" call. In a traditional "code blue" call, the team swoops in and takes over management of the patient. In contrast, successful RRTs say that their goal is to support and help the primary nurse. To demonstrate that in metrics, average RRT call durations are between 20–50 minutes, with most hospitals reporting an average call of around 30 minutes.

Also, to emphasize this goal, teams—particularly those that do not include a physician—encourage and sometimes mandate that the primary nurse make the call to the attending physician. Steering clear of designating this role to the RRT avoids the perception that a transfer in care and responsibility has occurred.

8. Articulate goals of the RRT

This step is important not only during implementation but also when designing your team. The major goals of a call should include the following:

- Plan to regroup and discuss the coordination and communication of the patient's status
- Specifically address the concern or criteria trigger that initiated the call
- Develop a plan that will be clear to the patient care team
- Patient will improve and not require a higher level of care transfer
- If a higher level of care transfer is required, it will be accomplished in a non-hurried, non-chaotic manner with an optimal hand-off of care

Education and other goals also may be included in this list. If you are communicating this list of goals well, there should be no confusion. Everyone, including the floor nurses, the members of the RRT, the ICU team, the code team, and the implementation team, should be able to articulate these goals.

9. Feedback is crucial

The two main goals of the rapid response team are to rescue and learn. In that vein, it is important to provide feedback to the units and the hospital in general. We will cover monitoring and sharing outcomes in the next chapter. For immediate feedback, do the following:

- Make it part of the RRT's role and responsibility to return to the unit for followup. Whether the patient stays on the floor or the follow-up visit is to provide information on the patient's condition at a transferred higher level of care, incorporating this structure will help with continued implementation. Ideally, this should be conducted as part of the routine, not just "if we have time."

- Celebrate the call. Hospital teams focusing on the learning aspect of the RRT have found their call numbers escalate quickly by returning to thank the unit for rescuing a patient that day. Some even distribute candy to the unit.

10. More complex than a recipe

Although we share many tips from other organizations, simply placing these strategies into your organization does not guarantee success.

In other words, it is not simply putting a recipe together, nor is it simply assembling various experts. A large portion of the true continued success of RRTs is understanding that it is really putting a system in place—and a complex one at that. Complex systems require attention to build individual relationship and to respond to those relationships. Brenda Zimmerman, PhD, in her research on complexity for healthcare leaders, compares complex systems to raising a child: Having the experience of raising one child successfully may help you with a second, but by no means can you expect the outcome to be like a recipe, where you get the same results every time.

What does that mean for your RRT? Here are a few recommendations:

- Carefully review your survey evaluations. Look in the comment sections for gems to review for changes within the system.

- Continue to care for and feed your rapid response system initiative. Don't expect to be able to implement in a short few weeks and walk away with success.

- Consider expanding relationships beyond those affected immediately by the direct intervention (e.g., the patient, floor nurse, and RRT members). Consider the effect on the attending, consulting, and cross-covering physician relationships; ED and ICU decisions on transferring patients; and laboratory and other services.

FIGURE 3.1 — SPECIFIC CONSIDERATIONS FOR SMALL HOSPITALS

Perhaps you are a small hospital—less than 150 beds—and you wonder whether the RRT concept applies to you. This question is understandable, especially considering the fact that all the peer review literature and many of the examples of RRTs in the field focus on large hospitals.

We believe that RRTs are just as important for small hospitals as large ones. However, here are a few considerations:

- Staffing challenges:
  - o If the 10 RRT calls per month per 100 beds estimate holds true in small hospitals, you will receive about 10–15 calls per month. With these numbers, it will be difficult to design a program with dedicated FTEs for the RRT program. However, think about building additional roles to complete the FTE job description, such as
    - clinical education role
    - ACLS/PALS/CPR education role
    - data collection and performance improvement (PI) role within the initiative

- Resistance to change:
  - o Although this issue is a challenge in all organizations, smaller and more geographically remote facilities may have a very stable and seasoned work force. Nursing turnover may not be a significant problem. Breaking down traditional hierarchies and demonstrating the advantage of removing those barriers will be more difficult. In addition, it is often from the new nursing graduates that we receive the most dramatic positive feedback for the RRT, so if you have very few new, your feedback may be more subtle.

- More emphasis on stories during early implementation:
  - o If your admission numbers are lower than those of the facilities previously mentioned in this book, you will not see the quick three- to four-month turnaround of your code data and mortality statistics. Your statistics are likely to return results more slowly and less dramatically. Keep the pressure on while you are monitoring these results with stories of RRT team rescue successes.

In our case studies, we have two hospitals featured from the Kaiser system and a Vermont facility— all of which have fewer than 200 beds. Read their stories to help put your implementation in the context of a smaller facility.

CHAPTER FOUR

MONITORING

CHAPTER FOUR

MONITORING

What indicators should an organization monitor? How much should it monitor? As with most performance improvement and system changes, measurement at some level is important to ensure that the change does, in fact, make a difference.

What you monitor and how much you monitor may depend in part on various resources available within your organization, including the manual and electronic capabilities of your organization to pull and review data.

Categories of measurements

The literature has provided some suggestions for measurement/monitoring points. We can divide them initially into four categories: "big picture" outcome measurements, "upstream" outcome measurements, process level measurements, and satisfaction measurements.

The categories break down as follows:

'Big picture' outcome measurements
Examples:

- Number of codes per 1,000 admissions
- Percentage of codes outside the ICU
- Mortality rates
- Survival rates of codes
- Length of stay (LOS) of patients after codes
- LOS of ICU patients
- Overall LOS
- Unplanned admissions to the ICU from the floor

- ED to ICU vs. floor to ICU LOS
- Percentage of deaths in the IHI's 2x2 matrix box D/4

These measurements look at overall outcomes. They do not include comparative severity adjustments and are not "benchmarked" between hospitals. Instead, they show an internal trend for improvement.

For example, without comparing the number of codes per 1,000 admissions, hospitals have internally shown remarkable drops in the number of codes (22%–75%) after implementing an RRT. Even more significantly, a drop in codes outside the ICU demonstrates improved rescue of patients as a result of the RRT. Importantly, these improvements often have been apparent within just a few months after implementation. And because several of the indicators listed above are likely to be already tracked by some review committee (e.g., code committee) within your hospital, few additional resources will be needed to take these measurements.

Process measurements

Examples:

- Number of RRT calls per month
- Percentage of calls resulting in transfer to a higher level of care
- Response time of RRT
- Primary criteria trigger for call
- Primary interventions
- Response time of physicians

Because outcomes can be affected by several causal factors—implementing an RRT being only one of them—process measurements are helpful to specifically focus on intermediate markers that reflect on the intervention. In particular, as the program grows and evolves, tracking these measurements can help you refine your program.

In general, we find an average of 10 calls per 100 beds per month around the United States for RRTs (or 15–25 calls per 1,000 admissions). The percentage of calls that result in transfer to a higher level of care ranges between 40% and 60%. Response-time goals for the RRT are often set for five minutes. If one of the gaps in process efficiency pre-RRT implementation has been identified as the primary physician response to a call on the unit, tracking the response may help identify system failures (e.g., centralized paging service, accurate identification of physician responsible). In addition, to improve response times relating to destabilizing situations associated with an RRT, some hospitals have created a paging code for the physician. For example, a suffix code such as *911* or *111* could be added to the end of a phone page to indicate that the call is urgent and requires a response within 10 minutes.

Many of these process measurements can be captured through an RRT call record. We have provided sample template used by one of our case studies (sample North Carolina Baptist Case Study).

'Upstream' outcome measurements

Examples:

- Number of postoperative myocardial infarctions on the floor per 1,000 surgical patients
- Number of acute renal failure patients per month
- Number of emergency intubations per month
- Relative use of palliative care services within the hospital

More specific learning may come from a closer look at adverse complications that are further upstream in a patient's care (that is, that precede the measure of a cardiac/respiratory arrest). Constantly ask whether more these complications can be avoided by timely intervention. A greater quality improvement focus as described in the previous chapter can result from following these important measures.

Michael Buist, MD, and his team of researchers at Dandenong Hospital in Australia found a significant role for its medical emergency teams in clarifying comfort care orders earlier. Bringing attention to this important decision point and clarifying it between the patient/family and care team was important in ensuring that the patient's desire and goals for care were communicated promptly.

Satisfaction measurements

Examples:

- Cultural survey results
- Nursing turnover rates
- Nursing satisfaction rates
- Physician satisfaction rates
- RRT call satisfaction results from the RRT
- RRT call satisfaction results from the calling floor/nurse

Call satisfaction between the RRT and the calling floor nurse can be captured by immediate survey (see sample form on p. 89). If your program has established administrative sponsorship and you have implemented leadership walkarounds on the floors, you can also gather feedback on satisfaction through interactions with staff during these conversations.

Physician satisfaction is important as well. Although many hospitals report overwhelming physician satisfaction with RRTs, it is crucial, particularly in your early implementation phase, to contact each attending physician that may have been affected by an RRT call. Were they aware that a new system was being piloted? Was the call helpful to them?

Indirect links to satisfaction through nursing turnover rates and safety culture surveys also have been key components in many organizations. Ultimately, providing a system that better supports the frontline worker reflects in overall staff retention.

Six tips for success

Here are some tips for successful monitoring of your RRT:

1. Clear the clutter

Don't get lost in the data. Measurements can provide interesting information and should not be ignored, but lengthy presentations with information cut at too many levels and perspectives will lose your audience. Therefore, separate, determine, and differentiate the data that are appropriate for each target audience. For example, Jewish Hospital (see case study) focused on mortality rates and number of codes as the primary two indicators that would be shared throughout the hospital, as well as with the hospital governance board.

2. Provide feedback frequently

How frequently? The hospitals interviewed for our case studies report that they often started by providing weekly feedback. After a period of time, they shifted to monthly feedback to keep attention on the project. This continued attention is important, as hospitals with less frequent feedback find awareness and interest waning after the initial "honeymoon period." They have seen a drop in the number of calls and have been challenged to sustain the momentum.

3. Use outcome measurements to build focus and drive

Before presenting outcome measurements to a group, put yourself in the audience's shoes. Be clear about where you are aiming with the measurements.

Summarize your results in the title of one or two clear graphical posters. For example, don't use dull titles such as

- "Rapid Response Call Utilization"
- "# Codes at Hospital X/1,000 admissions"

Instead, announce the findings in the title:

- "Rapid Response Call Utilization Jumps 25% between July and November"
- "Codes drop 33% in the first four months of Rapid Response Team Implementation"

4. Select measurements to learn

Remember that the primary purpose of monitoring and measurement is learning. The data is not meant to judge one team against another or one medical/surgical unit against another. Rather, the purpose is to prevent serious adverse events by getting the most appropriate expertise to the bed-side in the most timely manner.

With each measurement you track, ask, "What can I learn from this measurement?" Learning through these indicators will allow thoughtful redesign of the system and remove any barriers that may be impeding such expediency.

5. Putting faces to names

We often hear that implementing an RRT has affected nursing relationships between ICU and floor nurses. We have heard that trust is improved and the affected staff better appreciate what it is like to be in the other's shoes. Hospitals are seeing improved job satisfaction results and lower nursing turnover rates. Indeed, particularly in large organizations, ICU and floor nurses have fallen into a work routine where they have little interaction. What interaction they have is often short and some-times contentious. RRT programs have facilitated collegiality and improved communication by put-ting faces to names and increasing interaction and feedback. Ultimately, trust and morale improves.

6. Celebrate the results

Don't let positive results go unrewarded. The full feedback loop of any performance improvement or change cycle doesn't stop with just a plan-do-check-act. Celebration shows an appreciation for hard work, demonstrates that the organization values the contribution, and helps support sustained results. At Jewish Hospital, a hospital board member offered a personal thank you on behalf of the board at its third-year RRT celebration (see case study).

CHAPTER FIVE

THE FUTURE

CHAPTER FIVE

THE FUTURE

What does the future hold for RRTs? The following immediately comes to mind, based on the success and lessons learned from our interviews and case studies:

1. Rapid response teams/systems will be required of hospitals

- In September 2005, the JCAHO announced that RRTs will be included in the proposed National Patient Safety Goals for 2007. It remains to be seen whether, in the future, every hospital will be asked to review the need for, implement, and monitor early intervention systems as part of accreditation. It is possible that having a RRT may be an expectation of acute care hospitals, much like Code Blue teams are today. Certainly, the data supporting the impact of these systems cannot be ignored.

2. Patients and families will be able to activate rapid response teams

- Encouraging patients to participate in their care is a common theme in patient safety. JCAHO launched its "Speak up" campaign, and the National Patient Safety Foundation unveiled its "Nothing About Me Without Me" campaign. Hospitals have placed "Stop the Line" policies in their organizations and included patients and families. Allowing patients or families to trigger a call will only further reinforce a hospital's commitment to making patients an important part of the healthcare team.

3. Establishing early warning criteria and systems for potentially destabilizing conditions

- Hospitals that have several months of RRT data find that despite having criteria and permission for nurses to call for concerns, some patients still fall through the cracks. "Nurses at the bedside tend to get one slot of information," reflects Nancy Kimmel, RPh, patient safety officer of Missouri Baptist Medical Center in St. Louis (see case study).

As a result, Missouri Baptist is building an early warning system using its computer system as an adjunct; the same physiologic criteria that triggers an RRT call creates rules in the computer logic. The screen will flash yellow or red alerts as certain thresholds are met, advising the nurse on the situation.

In the future, hospitals may program computer systems not just for single threshold triggers but for trend-based triggers as well. Graphical displays over time and weight-based triggers could calculate global scores and alert staff to potential dangerous and destabilizing patterns in a patient's course.

Specific examples

- Early warning tools on admission. This type of system could identify higher-risk access patients as they come into the hospital and could provide an added safety net for their care (see Calgary case study).

- Early warning tools relating to delirium. Recent work by Wes Ely, MD, a pulmonologist at Vanderbilt University, suggests that ICU patients with delirium have longer lengths of stay. He has implemented and validated a modification of the original Confusion Assessment Method (CAM) tool that he developed with Sharon Inouye, MD, MPH. This modification is known as the CAM-ICU tool. For RRTs, adding delirium criteria may provide earlier recognition and intervention to destabilizing clinical situations.

- Early warning tools relating to neurologic status. Review of pre-code cases and floor nurse interviews of RRT cases has found that a "change in neuro status" can often trigger that "gut feeling." Perhaps a closer look at earlier identification and treatment of neurologic changes—particularly for medication induced reversible causes—will be another way to get the expertise in a particular subspecialty to the bedside in a timely manner to improve overall patient outcome.

UK experience

- The idea of early warning tools is not new. In the United Kingdom, several hospitals have worked with single-parameter, double-parameter, and multiple-weighted parameter scoring systems. The Department of Health and Modernization Agency in the UK offers the following guidelines to consider the following when implementing such tools:

What they are not

- Physiological track and trigger warning systems are not
  - o substitutes for clinical judgment
  - o predictors of the inevitable development of critical illness
  - o predictors of overall outcome from critical illness
  - o comprehensive clinical assessment tools
  - o indicators for immediate admission to ICU or HDU (high dependency unit)

What they are

- Physiological track and trigger warning systems are
  - o aids to good clinical judgment
  - o red flag markers of potential or established critical illness
  - o generally sensitive depending upon their complexity
  - o aids to effective communication in care of the critically ill and a means of securing appropriate help for sick patients
  - o indicators of physiological competence
  - o indicators of physiological trends
  - o valuable even in the absence of a formal critical care outreach service

The critical care outreach service that the agency mentions is an early form of the RRT concept.

4. Using the RRT information for performance improvement and education

- As clusters of cases occur, hospitals find that review of rapid response cases in aggregate can provide ideas for clinical care improvement. For example, many hospitals find that Systemic Inflammatory Response Syndrome and early sepsis are conditions with delayed diagnosis. Early goal-directed therapy has improved the outcome of these patients. Educating RRT members and physicians in the earlier recognition and consideration of sepsis as a potential differential diagnosis improves delivery of timely care.

- In another instance, a hospital found that a cluster of cases requiring RRT intervention with volume resuscitation was occurring on its acute oncology ward. The result was a decrease in the incidence of acute renal failure complications. Presenting this data to a multidisciplinary group of stakeholders, including the department chief of oncology, led to service-specific protocols that allowed for earlier intervention. In addition, nursing staff said the system improved anticipation and comfort level of these common-cause symptoms and treatment needs for their patients.

- If you have kept your medical staff quality committee/medical executive committee in the loop from the very beginning, you already will have hit the ground running to make these farther-reaching clinical care improvements.

5. Bringing appropriate expertise and necessary intervention to the bedside faster.

- This is the system goal of the RRT. It is not a specific best team or a turf battle of "who does what:" It is the recognition that in a highly complex and specialized healthcare system, each patient may require specific or unique expertise at any given time. To do so, answer the following questions:
  - Does our system recognize and facilitate this?
  - How?
  - Where are the delays?
  - Does everyone know where and how to activate appropriate resources in a timely manner?
  - Can patients and family activate these resources?

Every organization and community has a wealth of expertise and resources, both hidden and obvious. For example, you may have specific pediatric or psychiatric expertise within your hospital that does not reach the patient in as optimal, collaborative, and timely a manner as possible.

In fact, we are likely to find that RRTs are just the beginning of how we introduce and redesign new methods for patient intervention and clinical assessment in the hospital and the healthcare system in general.

FIGURE
5.1

EXPAND THE RRT CONCEPT TO MEET OTHER NEEDS

Consider the goal of ensuring more timely recognition, assessment, and treatment of medical conditions while a patient is in the hospital, as well as the acknowledgement that we often fail in this regard because of the complexity of the system and the patient. It is not a huge jump to consider other teams similar to the RRTs described in this book.

For example, do you have

- patients on your medical floors with potentially destabilizing psychiatric conditions?
- psychiatric patients in your units with potentially deteriorating medical conditions?
- pediatric patients that are not on a pediatric-specific unit?
- third-trimester patients admitted for acute illnesses in hospital units other than your labor and delivery unit?

All of these are situations in which a specialty nurse or specialty response team could be accessed for quick consultation, assessment, and coordination of timely interventions. These interventions also may lead to improved nurse-to-nurse collegiality in these dissimilar specialties. These teams may require the development of early recognition tools to help guide clinicians toward recognizing red flags of deterioration. As with RRTs, the focus of these specialty teams would be to better serve patient needs.

APPENDIX A

CASE STUDIES & FORMS

Note: The following case study is adapted from an HCPro audioconference entitled Rapid Response Teams: Field-tested Strategies to Implement Lifesaving Teams. *For more information on how to purchase an audiocassette of the program, call HCPro customer service at 800/650-6787.*

Baptist Memorial Hospital is a 736-bed acute care, non-teaching facility. It has 27,000 discharges and 50,000 emergency department visits annually.

Baptist Memorial determined that it needed a medical response team (MRT) after reviewing a series of cardiac arrests, says **Michelle Peck, RN**, head nurse of the hospital's intensive care unit (ICU). An in-house resuscitation team reviewed 429 consecutive cardiac arrests, which revealed immediate death, successful resuscitation, hospital death after successful resuscitation, and "failure to rescue" opportunities.

"We did literature search that showed acute illness is often missed and that ICU admissions might be averted by more adequate pre-ICU response," Peck says.

Two-member team

The team consists of an ICU float charge nurse and lead respiratory therapist. From 6 p.m. to 7 a.m., an intensivist on duty also will respond when needed. Any member of the hospital staff could call the MRT using suggested trigger criteria. "We've had calls from hemodialysis, therapy, express admission, literally all over the hospital," Peck notes.

A major goal of the MRT program was to facilitate the early intervention and stabilization of patients to prevent clinical deterioration or arrest, Peck says. In addition, the MRT encourages the development of critical thinking skills and confidence in staff members before a critical event occurs.

Criteria listed on posters

Baptist Memorial's MRT criteria are as follows:

- Staff member is worried about patient
- Acute change in heart rate
- Acute change in systolic blood pressure
- Acute change in respiratory rate
- Acute change in oxygen saturation
- Acute change in level of consciousness

The criteria were listed on posters, which were displayed prominently throughout the hospital, Peck says.

Quick turnaround

A three-day trial of the MRT was held, with the following results:

- The team received 10 calls from eight different units
- Six out of 10 MRT patients were admitted to the ICU
- Three of the 10 remained in their floor unit, and a follow-up visit was made by the MRT
- In one case, when aggressive respiratory treatment was initiated, the patient's husband made an end-of-life decision for the patient
- Three patients were intubated
- Four patients were started on vasoactive drips
- Three central lines were placed
- The average response time was less than five minutes
- The average time spent with the patient was 45 minutes

The MRT educated staff before the trial about the team and how and when to call it, Peck says. "We didn't set any parameters on our criteria," she adds. "We didn't want staff to have to decide whether to make the call [based on a number]; we wanted them to call."

To make the MRT concept work, the team needed to be accessible. The team pager number—1234—was simple to remember and was printed on cards that were handed out to staff throughout the facility, Peck says.

Peck said the team took the pilot data and analyzed it for each case, discussed opportunities with staff, and presented the data to administration and the medical staff. The presentation included one slide per patient and discussed the outcomes of all 10 patients the MRT assessed. The administration and medical staff were pleased with the results and decided to implement the program the following Monday, "which was pretty quick for us," Peck says. "We had to make sure we had the staff buy-in, the doctors' buy-in, and everybody on board with this."

The team was activated in August 2003. Initially, calls to the MRT often came in late, but that changed as staff grew more familiar with the team, Peck says.

Sample MRT call

The following is an example of one of the initial MRT calls:
- The patient had a change in respiratory status, with a decrease in oxygen saturation
- The patient had been hospitalized for nine months, with an order for "no chest compressions"
- The MRT assessed and prepared to intubate after consulting with the patient's physician
- The MRT explained the treatment plan
- The patient's husband said his wife "did not want all of this"
- The patient was placed on 100% non-rebreather AFM, oxygen saturation level came up
- The husband's wishes were expressed to the attending physician through the MRT
- The do-not-resuscitate order was received, the family called, a palliative care nurse was consulted for comfort care, and the patient died with her family present in the room

Staffing issues

Adjusting to the MRT rotation was difficult at first, Peck says. "We had to bite the staffing bullet in the unit," she adds. "The staffing ratio was one nurse to two or three patients, and since the program was in place, we had to use our own staff. There were a lot of unhappy nurses in the beginning." As the MRT program progressed and staff saw the results, however, the mood grew more positive.

Results

After the first few months of the MRT, Baptist Memorial saw the following results:
- The volume of codes went down by 25%
- The location of codes shifted. Previously, about 60% of codes occurred outside of critical

care, which meant that the patient was not in the highest level of care when the code occurred. Now, only 40% of the codes take place outside of critical care.

For the 12 months from October 2003 to September 2004, Baptist Memorial had 235 fewer deaths of Medicare patients than expected, Peck says. Of 15,275 discharges, there were 854 actual deaths compared to an expected total of 1,091.

Team uses SBAR sheet

After the MRT responds, the team does a full assessment of the patient, decides whether patient is critical and needs to be moved to ICU, and gathers a complete picture of the patient's condition before to calling the attending physician. The team fills out an assessment sheet that uses the SBAR (situation, background, assessment, recommendation/response) communication tool (see next page for a sample assessment sheet. The sheet is given to the physician upon his or her arrival on the scene.

FIGURE

1

TEAM CALL RECORD

Medical Emergency Team Call Record

Event Date: _____   Code Status _____   Patient Label

Admit Date: _____   Time called: _____

Arrival time: _____   End time: _____

Staff responding: _____

Staff initiating call _____

Primary Reason for MRT Call

Respiratory Status Change	Change in HR	Change in LOC	Change in BP	Staff Worried	Chest Pain	Fluid Status
<12 >28 SOB O2 sat:	>130 <40 rhythm:	lethargic confused unresponsive agitated/restless	<90 >170 undetectable	not look right unable get MD What's wrong?	new recurring	I>O wet lungs UOP<50cc/4hrs

Situation:

Background:

Assessment:

Recommendation/Interventions:

Patient Outcome: Stayed on Floor: ____   Transfer to ICU: ____   Code Blue: survived   expired

Follow-up 12 hour after event:

Source: Baptist Memorial Hospital, Memphis

The Calgary Health Region (CHR) provides healthcare services to 1.1 million residents in Southern Alberta and tertiary services to 1.3 million residents. The critical care department has three adult intensive care unit (ICU) sites, which admit more than 3,000 patients per year:

- Foothills Medical Center: Trauma/neuro multisystem ICU, 24 beds
- Peter Lougheed Centre: Multisystem ICU, 12 beds
- Rockyview General Hospital: Multisystem ICU, 10 beds

The CHR is part of the Canadian Critical Care Patient Safety Collaborative, which launched in the spring of 2003. One of the collaborative's goals for 2004-05 is to reduce in-hospital cardiac arrests by 50% using rapid response teams.

Team focuses on early recognition of problems

The CHR created an ICU outreach team to help staff on the patient care units with early recognition and management of patients at risk for developing critical illness, says **Ann Kirby, MD, FRCPC, MSc,** quality improvement physician for the CHR's critical care department and an associate professor at the University of Calgary.

The idea for the team came after reading studies from Australia and the United Kingdom on medical emergency teams and after the CHR experienced some problems of its own. "We had a couple of critical incidents that highlighted that this was a concern," Kirby says. In both cases, patients experienced harm or death that was avoidable; their care was mismanaged on the patient care units, and they ended up in the ICU too late.

Pilot team launched in February 2004

As a result, the CHR assembled a pilot "ICU outreach team" at Rockyview General Hospital. This team includes a respiratory therapist, registered nurse from the ICU, and a senior resident or physician of equivalent level. Team development took place from October 2003 to January 2004; education began in December 2003. The pilot project began February 2, 2004, and ran through July 31, 2004.

The team's roles and responsibilities are as follows:

- Physicians must attend every "code 66" within five to 15 minutes.

- Physicians assess the patient, then ensure and coordinate all diagnostic and therapeutic measures for optimal patient care. They communicate this assessment to the patient's attending team.

- The RT and RN must assess, diagnose, and guide the patient's healthcare team to carry out treatment as per physician's orders.

- The RT and RN work collaboratively with the patient's care team, ensuring clear communication and sharing of knowledge.

- The RT and RN support the ward staff in assessment and management of the patient.

Outreach criteria are as follows:

- Threatened airway
- Respiratory rate <5>36
- Pulse <40>140
- SBP <90
- Sudden fall in LOC—GCS of 2 or more; prolonged or repeated seizures
- Any patient about whom you are seriously worried

Training on concept and criteria

The CHR trained the ICU staff on the concept of the outreach team, but more time was spent training the rest of the facility staff on the following, says Kirby:

- Calling criteria
- Team criteria
- How to access the team
- Calling code "66"
- What to expect when the team arrives

Kirby says there was some resistance to the team, but not a lot. "We actually anticipated that we'd get more pushback," she adds. "We only had one service that resisted. We explained that the team was here to provide a safety net."

In addition, administration provided ample support for the education effort. "We tried to go through all departments to explain why we were doing what we were doing, not to ask permission," says Kirby.

The team's implementation resulted in a 40% reduction in cardiac arrests for the six-month period of the pilot, she says. During the first year that the team was in place, cardiac arrests were down 19%.

In addition to the patient safety improvement, the facility also looked at hospital days saved for cardiac arrest survivors and ICU days saved for cardiac arrest survivors. "Most of the patients that we see don't end up coming to the ICU, hopefully preventing ICU admissions," Kirby says.

The CHR now plans to add ICU outreach teams in the other two of its three facilities.

Electronic early warning system

The CHR also is integrating the ICU outreach team criteria into its electronic health record system to establish a modified early warning system, says Kirby. "We're determining which patients are at risk upon admission," she adds.

Two major signs for staff to watch are respiratory rate and urine output, so staff is being trained to understand the importance of these factors and to pay closer attention to them.

How are floor nurses responding to the four-month-old implementation of a rapid response team (RRT) at Hoag Memorial Hospital Presbyterian? "I go to our Starbucks cart on campus and nurses will come up to me telling me how thrilled they are to have this new resource," says **Paul Curry, MD**, anesthesiologist and Hoag's incoming chief of staff.

Preimplementation journey

Hoag's journey began in 2003 when Curry challenged the organization to acknowledge that "we could do a lot better recognizing when things go wrong and getting the right person to the bedside in timely fashion," he says.

Curry found that "although much of what we do managing patient care is predictable and amenable to structured policy and procedure, these same policies can drastically slow us down when the less probable strikes, often catching us unprepared."

He suggests that a parallel process needs to exist: 1) a policy-driven process and 2) a highly reliable sense-making process. "Optimal sense-making in emergencies means understanding that different nurses and different physicians bring different expertise to the table," he says. "A collaborative mindset is needed to get the most appropriate person to the bedside as quickly as possible. More and more disease states over the last 20 years have been recognized as deadly clocks ticking away, and rapid recognition and resuscitation is essential to mitigate morbidity."

The clincher came when Curry compared outcomes of Hoag's patients that were transferred to the ICU directly from the ED versus patients transferred to the ICU from the medical/surgical floors. "We saw twice the overall hospital mortality and twice the length of stay in our floor transfers compared to our ED transfers," he notes. As a result, the hospital's medical executive committee unanimously approved moving forward with a program. The data also helped bring board members, administrators, and other physicians on the medical staff together to make the RRT initiative happen.

A collaborative team

Initially, the program was thought to be a manpower-neutral initiative. All resources needed for support would come from those resources being saved from not having to respond to more extreme clinical problems/prevented cardiac arrests. In addition, part of the team consists of some members of Hoag's code blue team.

The hospital's core RRT includes an experienced ICU nurse, an experienced respiratory technician, and the nurse at the bedside, with an intensivist available when necessary. The three-person core description reinforces the "collaborative" concept, with the bedside nurse continuing to be integral to the care of the patient even after the RRT is called.

Curry also reinforces the educational component of the intervention. "This team is as much a knowledge ambassador, here to enhance the competencies of our med/surg nurses, as it is a rapid resource for intervention," he says. "We encourage our nurses to call the team even with the faintest intuitive discomfort concerning their patients."

What happens on a call

Basically, the following three scenarios can happen when a call is made:

- Scenario A: The team determines that no intervention needs to occur. If this happens and then eight to 12 hours later, the nurse again feels that "something's not right" and calls the RRT, a second assessment is made. If again no intervention is instituted, there's an automatic visit by the ICU/RT duo four hours later, regardless of whether the floor nurse calls again. As a courtesy to the attending physicians, they are notified on later rounds if the RRT calls were deemed "false alarms."

- Scenario B: The patient is near death when the team arrives. If this happens, the 24/7 hospital intensivist (the fourth team member) is immediately called to back up and assist in the management of the patient. These cases are usually imminent codes.

- Scenario C: The patient requires some level of intervention. After the assessment, the team calls the primary attending physician. If there is no response within 10 minutes, the intensivist is called. If the primary attending calls after the intensivist has responded, the two physicians continue discussion and collaborate on management of the case.

The RRT has certain protocols and interventions that it can institute without a physician order as well, including volume resuscitation, handheld respiratory treatments, and intubation. Interventions such as starting vasoactive drips require a physician order.

Lessons learned so far

"We realized that many of us had unfortunately conditioned our nurses over the years to never call for help unless absolutely sure something was wrong," says Curry. In its early implementation phase, Hoag Hospital abandoned any hard, physiologic criteria for calling the RRT. "We felt it was more important to rid ourselves of this destructive 'waiting' behavior, and that using hard criteria might only reinforce more 'waiting' rather than encouraging our nurses to develop and rely on their intuition."

Not surprisingly, the first month's results reflected what Curry refers to as the RRT's "100% 'positive predictive value."

"All the calls were patients in extreme need, and I wanted us to get to the patients much, much earlier," he adds. "Since this team is as much about teaching as it is intervention, we set a new goal for a 40% positive predictive value—meaning only 40% of patients should actually require any kind of intervention."

Although the hospital's program has not met this new goal, it has dropped the need for patient transfers to an ICU from 100% down to 40%.

Curry also cautions those putting an RRT in place to ensure open and "decentralized" communication during design and implementation. He points out that all staff involved—the floor nurse, intensive care nurse, or respiratory technician—need to have a safe forum to express their needs and vision. The goal of the RRT from one perspective may be different from that of another.

Hoag has also reexamined the hard physiologic criteria that the program chose to drop during early RRT implementation. The facility recently instituted some of those "end-point" hard physiologic criteria that explicitly require an RRT call. One of the advantages to reestablishing the criteria is that doing so encourages a call even if a physician is already in attendance. "This change allows all our patients to benefit from the collaborative help of an intensivist, should certain critical physiologic parameters be reached, regardless of whether another physician may already be involved," says Curry.

The future: Ensuring resiliency

Hoag has many other early "restabilization" initiatives underway. There is an early goal-directed sepsis initiative, and there are early stroke and epilepsy initiatives. The early recognition of sepsis has already been incorporated into the education of the RRT members. There are plans underway to have the team trained in epilepsy and stroke management. As a result of these multipronged initiatives, Hoag's administration has recently approved the addition of a 24/7 "flex-nurse" position, equivalent to 4.6 FTEs. This will provide the human resources needed for these initiatives to operate effectively.

INTEGRIS BAPTIST MEDICAL CENTER, OKLAHOMA CITY

"It all started when we asked ourselves, 'Do we have too many codes?' " says **Shirley Dearborn, MD**, administrative medical director of graduate medical education at INTEGRIS Baptist Medical Center. The 480-bed hospital, although not an academic medical center, is a tertiary referral hospital with residency programs, and has the highest acuity rate of any hospital in the state. The facility boasts one of the country's top solid organ transplantation programs; it also treats significant populations of high-acuity cardiac, end-stage renal disease, and burn patients.

Dearborn's team conducted a detailed review of 81 codes over a four-month period. The review included an assessment of each patient's clinical status prior to the code, including vital signs; various laboratory studies, nursing concerns, etc.; interventions provided; the patients' status after the codes; and opportunities for early intervention.

Although INTEGRIS performed its review before most medical emergency team and rapid response team (RRT) studies were published, the team found that their measurements of mental status, vital sign changes, and nursing concerns were similar to those in the literature.

"We then conducted multidisciplinary case reviews that staff, residents, and physicians could attend," recounts Dearborn. "One of the nurses who went to a review could not believe her staff could miss this stuff. 'What can we do?' she asked us."

Make way for DUCS

Pediatric intensivist **Johnny Griggs, MD**, nurse manager **Darsi Landsberger** (who later volunteered her floor to pilot the program), and Dearborn developed an educational process for nursing, respiratory therapy, and other staff concerning shock and the abnormal vital signs and mental status changes that should trigger more intense review of the patient.

Landsberger christened the project "DUCS," which stands for "Discovering Underlying Clinical Symptoms." The acronym provided an easy focus for the project.

"Dr. Griggs gave inservices on the pathophysiology and recognition of shock," says Dearborn. "He said over and over, 'If it looks like a duck, walks like a duck, quacks like a duck, it's a duck. Shock is shock.'"

The abnormal vital signs and mental status changes of shock were placed on laminated pocket cards for easy reference. Staff members now carry "DUCS cards" routinely. Whoever identifies a patient with these signs calls another nurse at a supervisory level, who also evaluates the patient and then calls the physician as appropriate. "It looks like we dropped the number of codes. And this is before we have developed a full response RRT program," Dearborn notes.

The most common interventions were oxygen administration, intravenous fluids, and transfusion. Some patients were transferred to the ICU.

The project, which has been largely a nursing intervention, will serve as a precursor to a more formal RRT program.

"We will formalize the program and make it more consistent, which will require more physician buy-in," Dearborn says. The "DUCS" program already has a track record for helping with clinical communications because physicians are getting better and clearer information from the nurses. But, she adds, "We don't want to derail the project with the MDs thinking the RRT program is taking over the care of the patient."

With the hospital's open ICU model, endorsement of the RRT program by the hospital's critical care committee is important. The committee includes pulmonologists, thoracic and cardiovascular surgeons, nephrologists, pediatric intensivists, ICU nurses, and respiratory therapists. Griggs and Dearborn recognized that with the open ICU model, the physicians had been accustomed to levels of autonomy and control that must be balanced to ensure RRT success.

RRTs approved for two hospitals

The measured and careful consensus development of the DUCS program has been rewarded. In the summer of 2005, the critical care, medical quality, and medical executive committees at both INTE-GRIS Baptist Medical Center and its sister facility, INTEGRIS Southwest Medical Center (also in Oklahoma City), approved the initiation of RRTs.

The new RRT will include an ICU nurse, a respiratory therapist, and a resident. The ICU nurse is the current "back-up code blue nurse." The respiratory therapist comes from the supervisory pool and has no patient assignments most of the time.

FIGURE
2

INTEGRIS Baptist Medical Center DUCS Criteria Card

DUCS List

Initial Review

If your patient has any of the following, contact:

Day shift: Team manager/clinical director

Evening shift, night shift, or weekends: Team manager/administrative supervisor

- Heart rate > 120 or < 50
- Systolic blood pressure < 90
- Respiratory rate < 10 or > 30
- Abnormal mental status
- Oxygen saturation < 90% despite oxygen therapy

Notify physician as appropriate.

Each patient should be evaluated at least once a shift

AND

At the time of any significant clinical change using the above criteria

- -

Team manager, clinical director, or administrative supervisor evaluation

If the patient has any of the following, contact as appropriate:

Attending physician

or

consultant physician

- Staff member is worried about the patient
- Acute change in heart rate to < 50 or > 120
- Acute change in systolic blood pressure to < 90
- Acute change in respiratory rate to < 10 or > 30
- Acute change in oxygen saturation to < 90%, despite oxygen therapy
- Acute change in mental status (conscious state)
- Acute change in urine output to < 50ml in 4 hrs

Record name, medical record number, and date of all patients identified using the above screen.

JEWISH HOSPITAL, LOUISVILLE, KY

Now into its third year of having a medical emergency team (MET) in place, officials at Jewish Hospital can step back and reflect on the difference made by the program.

"The day we went live, we might as well have gone hospitalwide," says **Joris Kramer, MSN, RN**, assistant vice president for critical care nursing at Jewish Hospital. The 442-bed hospital includes a 47-bed ICU, a 14-bed open heart unit, and 151 intermediate-level beds.

No physician resistance

Physicians quickly supported the program. "We have MDs who start the call," Kramer says. "They will say, 'Call the MET team and get their input.'" The hospital has 515 physicians on its active medical staff, and it continues to receive unsolicited positive feedback.

Additionally, the ED physicians who used to answer many of the floor calls before the advent of the MET system found that the program kept them from being pulled away from the ED.

Also, "It is important that we have a physician administrator—our VPMA—who is extremely supportive of this effort," adds Kramer.

Data collection and outcomes

The need for a new system became evident in 2002, when a review of data revealed that more than 60% of codes occurred outside of the ICU. Much like literature data, Jewish Hospital officials felt that pre-ICU care needed improvement. "We wanted to get the expertise and technology to the patient, regardless of location, within minutes."

The hospital set two prominent goals:

- Decrease the incidence of in-hospital codes
- Decrease patient mortality rates

Although the team collects a lot more data to help it understand where the program works well and where it can be improved, focusing on two major data points keeps the rest of the medical center and the board clear on the priorities.

In fact, the number of codes outside the ICU has dropped by more than 30%, and the quarterly tracking of patient mortality rates over the past three years has demonstrated clear trends downward.

Jewish Hospital celebrates its MET success with a recognition dinner. Kramer has invited a board member to be a champion from the very beginning. At the latest dinner, this board member was able to personally extend congratulations and appreciation from the board to the members of the MET initiative.

The team and training

The team at Jewish Hospital consists of two ICU unit charge nurses and a respiratory therapist. There is no physician on the team. The charge nurses do not have other patient care responsibilities, but between the two of them, there is a shared understanding and awareness of the hospital's moment-to-moment bed and capacity situation. Therefore, if it becomes clear that the patient will require a transfer, these two key individuals who would help [edits okay?] move other patients are already present and able to begin that discussion.

At the time of the program initiation, the hospital—which does not have a closed intensivist model—had begun an ICU course for its physicians. It used the Society of Critical Care Medicine's Fundamental Critical Care Support course. "We sent our ICU charge nurses and respiratory therapists to the course, as well," says Kramer. "It was excellent training for them."

What the team does

"'What can I do while I'm on the MET?' was a question we got from our charge nurses," says Kramer. What MET nurses found was that they could ensure that the patient had a patent IV site at the time of recognized instability. As a result, the team carefully put together a soft-sided duffel bag of equipment that it carries to the calls. The items are color-coded and consist mainly of IV equipment, portable BP, portable oxygen, and a Doppler cuff.

The early calls

"We implemented the MET team with a pretty strict [set of] criteria to start with," recalls Kramer. "But within a year, we saw the value of encouraging the staff to just call if you have a concern. We wanted to make sure that the nurse never felt bad about making a call."

The program now receives about 44 calls per month, which is close to the fairly standard 10 calls per month per 100 beds.

Unfounded concerns

Initial fears about the program proved unfounded, Kramer says. "I thought [the MET program] would overwhelm my ICU, but it did not," she says. Approximately 40% of the calls result in the patient staying on the floor, with the remaining 60% moving to intermediate- or ICU-level care.

"I was also worried that I would be taking my charge nurses off their units for three to four hours at a time," continues Kramer. In fact, the average MET call is 50 minutes. The team emphasizes to the nurses that it is not meant to jump in and take over. The team is there to support and learn from floor staff, she adds.

FIGURE 3

IMPLEMENTATION & RESULTS OF A MEDICAL EMERGENCY TEAM

Patient Label

Jewish Hospital MET Documentation Form

Date: _____ Time: _____

Patient/room#: _____
Criteria for call: _____ Call 777 if you have a concern about patient's condition

What alarmed patient's nurse? _____ Respiratory distress, threatened airway, change in breathing pattern

_____ Acute change in BP, HR
_____ Acute change in LOC
_____ Decreased urine output without history of renal dysfunction
_____ New, repeated or prolonged seizures
_____ Failure to respond to treatment

Call appropriate: _____Yes _____No

Action taken: _____ None needed

Other: _____
_____

Did you have everything you needed? _____ Yes _____No

Patient outcome:
_____ Patient stabilized with protocol intervention only
_____ Patient stabilized after call to MD for order
_____ Patient required transfer to higher level of care prior to any action
_____ Patient required transfer to higher level of care after intervention
_____ Patient coded
_____ Patient expired

Level of care from:	Level of care to:
_____ M/S	_____ Interm
Interm	ICU

Physician involvement:
_____ Physician notified
_____ Intervention/orders appropriate

Other: _____
_____
ICU RN amount of time off unit: _____

To be filled out by Nursing Administration only:
Patient discharge :
Date: _____
Outcome : _____
Source: Jewish Hospital, Louisville, KY. Reprinted with permission.

Overseeing patient safety for all 29 hospitals in the Kaiser Permanente California health system, Patient Safety Director **Suzanne Graham, RN, PhD**, has been instrumental in the organization's leadership effort to make patient safety an integral part of its delivery of care.

"In three or four years, rapid response teams [RRT] will be a way of life," she predicts. "We won't even have to talk about it."

Patient safety culture is key

Laying the foundation for the right culture and bringing patient safety education to the front line has been a goal for Graham and for Kaiser leadership. She believes strongly that all their project initiatives—including RRTs—will be more successful with this foundation. This culture effort has been part of Kaiser's quality and safety journey since 2000, and with the release of the Institute of Medicine's 1999 report, *To Err is Human*, Kaiser kicked its patient safety focus into higher gear.

"It started with efforts to develop responsible reporting," says Graham. "Each hospital put in place a policy and procedure, and all hospitals conducted an assessment of their environment with an eight-item safety attitude questionnaire. Current work is ensuring that action plans that were put in place are working—a follow-up assessment will be done at the end of 2005."

Human factors education also plays an important role, she continues. The organization has six modules in its human factors education:

- Briefings
- Debriefings
- Situational awareness
- Assertiveness
- Communication and teamwork
- Walkarounds

"RRTs use all of these concepts," says Graham.

With hospitals in various stages of RRT implementation, Graham cites several critical success factors for implementation. These include but are not limited to the following:

- Picking the team: Certain skill competencies are important. However, it is equally if not more important that the team have good communication and education skills and that it respond in a positive manner so that nurses are likely to call again. "The nurses have to like the team they will be calling," she says. "These teams need to answer with a smile and understand how important the education process is to the call."

- Integrating SBAR into the initiative: "SBAR is key to these programs," Graham says.

- Having measurable outcomes established at the onset.

When asked what the next few years might hold for RRTs, Graham raises the following questions: "How does the nursing staff ratio have an impact on this? Will there be fewer calls with the new requirements? Do hospitalist-based medical centers have an equal need for RRTs? How best do we collaborate with union partners to make these programs happen?"

These questions may be answered as the RRTs throughout Kaiser Permanente are implemented and evaluated. In the meantime, however, here are two case studies from the Kaiser Permanente Hospital System:

Kaiser Permanente-Roseville (CA) Medical Center

An RRT program can work in a smaller hospital, says **Charles Meek, RN**, nurse manager at Kaiser Permanente-Roseville Medical Center. The 166-bed facility has had a RRT in place for about a year. "At 2 a.m., a patient might begin to deteriorate and need additional assessment. A call would be made to our in-house hospitalist, but that person would be busy in the emergency room," says Meek.

"Our team consists of our ICU charge nurse and a respiratory therapist," Meek says. "We used the concept of rapid cycle testing to put this program in place. It went from being just a small test that grew and never went away."

In the hospital's initial cost-benefit analysis, the facility chose not to add the financial resources to fund more staff for the program. As it turns out, the hospital gets an average of 12 calls per month, which is "very doable," Meek says.

Kaiser Roseville's goal is to have the team respond within 10 minutes and to be at the bedside for no more than 20 minutes. In fact, the team currently responds within five minutes. A house supervisor also attends the call and begins to work on finding a bed for the patient at the same time.

The critical lessons that Meek would share with other hospitals include the following:

- Education: Specifically, educate staff prior to implementation. "Although we did a lot of education up-front on the floors, there was still confusion after implementation on when to call, who was to show up, and the roles of the members."

- Feedback: Specifically, tell stories. Meek regularly encourages staff to tell RRT success stories at staff meetings. He also sends a survey after each call. The combination of these efforts brings information back to the frontline staff and "they really feel they can prevent codes."

- Challenges of a stable work force: Being a small hospital with veteran staff, Meek found that despite the education and feedback, there appears to be some resistance in using the team. As the hospitalists slowly buy in to the benefits of the team, Meek envisions adding a hospitalist to it and believes that this addition may encourage more calls from the experienced staff.

Meek and his team hoped to lower the number of unplanned transfers to the ICU. After the RRT had made 119 calls, they have found that only 42 transferred to the ICU. Meek reports monthly statistics on the ICU transfer rate, utilization rate, and the number of codes into and out of the ICU. In the first four months, Kaiser Roseville saw a 23% reduction in the number of codes outside the ICU.

Kaiser Sunnyside Medical Center, Portland, OR, area

"I'm an emergency room physician, so I know that that there are times when I walk into a room, I see a patient and think to myself, 'This does not look good,' " says **Amy Lawrence, MD**, physician director of patient safety for the Northwest Region. "I know that all clinicians use their gut feeling." The 185-bed facility was in the planning stages of its RRT implementation in August 2005.

Because it is a smaller hospital, one of Kaiser Sunnyside's challenges has been determining how and who to staff for its RRT. "We wanted to use our hospitalists, but with the hospital often running at 95% occupancy, everyone was concerned that the coverage might not be consistent and they might get swamped," says Lawrence.

Therefore, Sunnyside has adopted the following strategies to help staff its RRT:

1) A two-tiered answering system:
  • The team will consist of an ICU nurse, an RT, and a hospitalist. The ICU nurse will respond within five minutes at the first tier. At the second tier, a hospitalist will respond if necessary within the next five minutes.

2) Funding for a half-time FTE coordinator:
  • This coordinator will help handle the data and also will be an RRT responder. "Most of all, the individual will beat the drum and be the face of the program," explains Lawrence.

Although there is plenty of momentum to start the program, Lawrence's work group is taking a measured pace. "We are anticipating a December 1 start date," she advises. In the meantime, Kaiser Sunnyside is part of a national collaborative of hospitals building RRTs, so there is much work and sharing being done. Some of those specifics include the following:
  • Establishing metrics to monitor the program
  • Defining the set of protocols that nurses can activate
  • Building more consistent physician involvement

Getting more physician involvement "has been our biggest struggle so far," Lawrence notes. "But my rationale to the hospitalists is that these are the very same patients you will be seeing in a code blue. This will be saving you work."

The future for RRTs is "incredible," according to Lawrence. "We are building a new system that culturally supports the nurse, doesn't beat the spirit down, raises the educational level, and is making the right resources available at the right time."

CASE STUDY	MERCY MEDICAL CENTER, DES MOINES, IA

In 2003, Mercy Medical Center reviewed three specific patient safety indicators:

- Unplanned returns of patients to the ICU
- Physician response time
- Nursing use of existing system resources

In its initial review, Mercy found that the baseline return rate was 3.9%. One unit that received a significant number of the ICU patients had a return rate of 7.8%, with 21 % of those patients returning within the first 24 hours and 54% returning within three days.

The review led to the pilot and eventual initiation of a rapid response team (RRT) in the 550-bed community referral hospital, says **Mary Brown, RN, MSN**, Mercy's patient safety officer and associate chiief for missing practice.

Staffing challenges

Staffing this program has been a challenge, as it is for most all programs. Mercy uses a physician-driven model during the day—"an expansion of our intensivist model," explains Brown—and a nurse-driven model in the evening. In addition, the house nursing supervisor may transfer a patient to a higher level of care (e.g., the ICU) without a physician order.

Three critical care nurses currently enrolled in a master's program are key champions to moving the program forward. "We didn't have the five full-time equivalent staff to add to the organization, and all of our charge nurses have a patient load," says Brown.

"In the pilot program, we freed up one of our critical care nurses in our master's program for 40 hours per week on the off shift," Brown adds. This implementation strategy allowed the hospital to test many aspects of the planned rapid response system.

"Now, our flight team—i.e., our paramedic nurses—are interested in being part of developing our RRT," Brown notes. "We also are looking at what we have done successfully in our neonatal transfer team model with nine transport nurses to identify what can work."

Certainly, using unique collaborative resources and reviewing existing "working" models can help you design an RRT that is successful in the context of each distinctive hospital structure.

To roll out the program beyond the pilot, Mercy created a job description for the RRT members. It allows the program to articulate clearly the expectations and skills that it seeks.

Two new initiatives

In addition, two other important initiatives are occurring at the same time at Mercy. The first is that the hospital, being part of the Keystone ICU collaborative on improving ICU care, has implemented a daily goals sheet to use not only during the ICU stay but also during hand-offs and transfers of patients from the ICU to step-down and floor units. A "transfer out checklist" is used by the ICU nurses to encourage "pausing to evaluate if the patient truly meets transfer criteria," explains **Monica Gordon,** patient safety coordinator at Mercy. In addition, a standing physician transfer order has been created which triggers specific nursing and respiratory therapy assessments during the first 48 hours after transfer.

The second initiative uses Six Sigma methodology, which the hospital has adopted, to explore improving reliability by adding a non-ICU float nurse who will increase the frequency of patient assessments on specific at-risk patient populations.

In combination with the RRT initiative, these "rescue" strategies have resulted in the percentage of unplanned returns to the ICU on their pilot 6N unit to drop from 7.8% to 4.3%.

Although the strategies have contributed to the overall measurement goal of reducing unplanned returns to the ICU, Brown says they also share a common focus: clearer communication.

CASE STUDY	MISSOURI BAPTIST MEDICAL CENTER, ST. LOUIS

Missouri Baptist Medical Center in St. Louis collaborated with its early adopter sister hospital in Memphis during the initial development stages of its rapid response team (RRT). The 489-bed community hospital's RRT is now in its second year, compiling an enviable track record with many lessons learned.

As of August 2005, Missouri Baptist's RRT had responded to more than 1,000 calls, says Performance Improvement Coordinator **Nancy Sanders, RN.**

Keys to success

Sanders outlines the following keys to success for the facility's RRT:

1. Having a core program to build on

"It really helped that we had a physician assistant [PA] program in place for 13 years. We built on that," says Sanders. The hospital's full RRT consists of a PA, an intensive care unit (ICU) nurse, and a respiratory therapist (RT). Prior to the RRT, the PA answered emergency (i.e., noncode) calls. The other two members have flexible schedules without specific patient assignments, enabling them to respond to calls. By bringing together a multidisciplinary team of clinicians, including Sanders' expertise in performance improvement, the initial task force asked, "What do we need to know when we get to a call?" The team developed a call record emerged to be focused and to clarify the clinical situation.

2. Delivering promptly

The hospital's RRT has a particularly enviable response time. Tracking this indicator, it can demonstrate a 90-second average response time.

3. Tracking all calls and providing frequent feedback

The hospital emphasizes constant feedback. "I send the [RRT] case reports back to each unit's nurse manager, every week," says Sanders. "This puts it back in their hands for immediate education."

Other feedback goes back to the medical executive committee and board levels through presentations by the chief medical officer. They receive presentation reports on the following:

- Number of calls per month
- Code rate
- Percentage of transfers to the ICU
- Survival rate after an RRT

Some of the more notable improvement statistics include a cardiac arrest rate that dropped 50% in just six months, and a 55% decline in emergency and respiratory arrest calls. Furthermore, in-hospital myocardial infarction rates have dropped an impressive 26% while monitoring the program, and the survival rate of those who experience a myocardial infarction has improved from 13% to 24%.

Patient Safety Officer **Nancy Kimmel, RPh,** another RRT champion for the hospital, notes, "One thing that opens everyone's eyes is the comparison of our survival rates after codes—which is between 18% and 21% versus the 81% survival rates after an RRT call." Although Sanders is the primary operational point lead, Kimmel's patient safety perspective also offers lessons of insight on implementation and feedback.

4. Being aware of the culture within the organization

"We took specific efforts to train our response teams as a group and had discussions on culture and hierarchy that existed within the hospital and medical profession," says Kimmel. The hospital also introduced SBAR (Situation, Background, Assessment, Recommendation/Response) training simultaneously on the units, encouraging rethinking of cultural hierarchy. Pre- and postimplementation cultural surveys over the previous year show specific improvements in nursing response.

Overcoming implementation challenges

Missouri Baptist advises the following steps to overcome implementation challenges:
- **Pilot small and gradual to address resistance quickly**

The hospital chose to trial its new system initially on a single unit during daytime hours, and then expanded it to 24 hours on that single unit prior to going hospitalwide.

By introducing the change on a small scale, Missouri Baptist was able to address resistance quickly as it occurred. For example, the hospital differentiated "rescue" versus "resuscitation" to highlight the differences between the RRT and the code team. The gradual ramp-up also emphasized the importance of having the team work together, train together, and be at the bedside together, compared to handling calls over the phone.

• Be aware of workarounds

"We began to find cases where the nurse would just call the PA and not call the RRT," cautions Sanders. Apparently, since the RRT call required a certain amount of documentation, staff sometimes avoided the paperwork by directly calling the PA.

"I review all those cases," Sanders adds. "The patients almost universally still get adequate care, but on occasion, the care gets delayed. The team would have been there in 1.5 minutes, whereas by calling the PA alone, the team ends up getting there several minutes later." Sanders uses cases as educational moments and reinforces her position that "we learn from every call."

• Build on your criteria

The team started with the traditional criteria published in Rinaldo Bellomo's Australian research. It added "staff member concerned" to the list but in its most recent evolution has added several other criteria. Specifically, "failure to respond to treatment for an acute problem/symptom" has been an important addition, says Sanders. "For example, if a patient receives a diuretic and one hour later is not any better, the RRT gets called right away instead of waiting four hours to meet the urine output criteria. We encourage staff to call in situations where there is a treatment plan to address a symptom or sign but the plan is not working."

Criteria for calling the rapid response team at Missouri Baptist Medical Center

- Staff member concerned/worried about the patient
- Acute change in heart rate (less than 40 or greater than 130 beats per minute)
- Acute change in systolic blood pressure (less than 90 mm/Hg)
- Acute change in respiratory rate (less than eight or greater than 24 breaths per minute) or threatened airway
- Acute change in blood oxygen saturation (SpO2 less than 90% despite oxygen)
- Fractional inspired oxygen (FiO2) of 50% or greater
- Acute change in mental status (delirium, confusion, etc.)
- Acute significant bleeding
- New, repeated, or prolonged seizures
- Failure to respond to treatment for an acute problem/symptom

---

- **Have a contingency plan**

Both Sanders and Kimmel emphatically caution all hospitals implementing an RRT system to develop a back-up plan. As the RRT initiative became more widely used in their organization, the teams found that they would sometimes receive 70–80 calls in a month. A backup plan should be in place to address how to deal with two simultaneous calls to the RRT, Kimmel says.

Having a backup plan may not be the first thing considered in early implementation of an RRT, but if the message is that the team will always be there and responsive in less than five minutes, such contingency plans should not be ignored.

Positive impact with stories

Sanders has a wealth of RRT rescue stories to share. "Just yesterday, we had a patient in the dialysis unit who became hypotensive and went on to have seizures," she says. "The RRT was called and was there within 1.5 minutes. Without this system in place, the dialysis team might have been much slower to call for help from a code team—it is always more difficult to call a 'Code 555' or cardiac arrest. In addition, we had a team of three show up instead of the entire [cardiac] code team, creating much less anxiety for the other patients."

Sanders also found the RRT system is an important rescue step for the hospital's outpatient and visitor population. For example, if a visitor passes out, an RRT call can be made. The team shows up and takes the patient to the ED. Because these visitors do not have a primary nurse assigned to them or attending physician of record, the potential chaos and delay of getting the patient to the ED can be significant. Instead, the RRT takes care of that by coming to the immediate and timely attention of the "visitor."

NORTH CAROLINA BAPTIST HOSPITAL, WINSTON-SALEM, NC

Note: The following case study is adapted from an HCPro audioconference, Rapid Response Teams: Field-tested Strategies to Implement Lifesaving Teams. For more information on how to purchase an audiocassette of the program, call HCPro customer service at 800/650-6787.

North Carolina Baptist Hospital is an 821-bed academic medical center that is part of the Wake Forest University Baptist Medical Center. In November 2003, the facility's quality of care committee determined that "failure to rescue" situations existed in the hospital because specialized care and some procedures were not available on general units, says **Becky Petree, RN, BSN, CNA-BC,** associate director of three of North Carolina Baptist's intensive care units (ICU) and coordinator of its rapid response team (RRT).

In addition, transferring patients to a higher level of care was often delayed because beds were not immediately available, she says.

The committee's research found that early recognition of patient deterioration followed by appropriate treatment could prevent failure-to-rescue situations, Petree notes. Failure to rescue affects patient satisfaction, length of stay, cost, and, most importantly, patient outcome.

The plan

A task force on failure to rescue was formed, and it developed a four-part plan to improve the hospital's rescue efforts, Petree says.

First, the hospital clarified its chain-of-command policy, which it felt was not strong enough. The policy was piloted in April 2004 and implemented facilitywide in September 2004.

The task force also developed a trigger tool of adult physiologic parameters that would be used to call in a rapid response team. The tool was developed and supported by nurses and physicians, and the task force educated staff about it. The tool also was tested in April 2004 and released facility-wide in September 2004 (see p. 85 for trigger tool.

The third step was to form a rapid response team, Petree says. First, the task force determined an area of focus, which centered on all medical/surgical inpatient units.

"We were looking at where most of our issues seemed to come from," Petree says. "We were having many patients returning to the ICU because of respiratory problems, so we felt that the inpatient med/surg units were certainly the hot spots."

After evaluating RRT models used at other hospitals, North Carolina Baptist chose critical care RNs who function under the direction of the patient's attending physician and the ICU policy, Petree says. Other disciplines provide support as needed.

Expansion of program under consideration

North Carolina Baptist implemented its RRT on October 17, 2004. At first, the team received 3.1 calls per day; six months later, it responded to 10.5 calls per day.

North Carolina Baptist is considering an expansion of the RRT to other areas such as clinics, radiology, or the outpatient comprehensive cancer center, adds Petree.

The team consists of six nurses, which means that there's one nurse on call for each 12-hour shift every day of the week. Petree says the hospital also may expand the size of the team, as in its first six months, the RRT saw 1,130 patients. North Carolina Baptist uses some of its critical care nurses as backup in emergency situations or when two calls come in at once, but primarily, the responding team is made up of one nurse, she adds.

The benefits of the team

The benefits of North Carolina Baptist's RRT are as follows:
- ICU care is taken to the patient until the patient is stabilized or is transferred to a higher level of care
RRT nurse is called when

-the trigger tool is implemented

-the activities of care require more resources than are available on the med/surg unit

-the activities of care exceed documented scope of RN assigned to the patient

-the staff is concerned or has a "gut feeling" about the patient's condition

- Specialized procedures and monitoring can be provided for a period of time outside the ICU
  These include

  -1:1 monitoring

  -conscious sedation

  -fluid bolus

  -medications and intravenous drips

  -assistance with procedures (CT insertion, central lines, etc.)

Transfer to higher level of care, arrest, and/or death may be prevented by providing early intervention

Early intervention can do the following:

  -Decrease length of stay in hospital

  -Decrease length of stay in the ICU

  -Decrease cost

  -Improve outcomes

Challenges

Some of the challenges presented by RRTs include the following:

- Education in a complex system

  -Multiple departments

  -Staff turnover

  -Ongoing role development for RRT as well as general nursing staff

- Staffing shortages

  -Experienced staff were recruited for start-up of RRT, which led to shortages in ICU

  -Turnover of team members

- Data collection
    - -The facility began with a manual system (see p. 84 for sample log which was cumbersome and time-consuming
    - -The MRT developed a computerized database, which it began using in March 2005.

- Communication
    - -Positive feedback is essential
    - -Updates on progress and issues to nurses, physician and administration
    - -Need to identify opportunities for improvement

Monitoring and measuring results

North Carolina Baptist uses a data collection tool that makes the process simple and inclusive, Petree says. Even though the facility is using a computerized database, the RRT still uses the log when it goes on calls to write a brief summary and later enter it into computer. "It is simple, but it is inclusive," she says.

The facility's benchmarking efforts measure outcomes, number of codes, length of stay, and transfers to a higher level of care.

| | | RRT Log | | | | | | | |

FIGURE 4

NORTH CAROLINA BAPTIST HOSPITAL
RRT LOG

DATE	TIME CALL RECD	CALLER MD/RN	PT NAME MR#	ROOM # ATTENDING	REASON FOR CALL	RESPONSE/DISPOSITION	TIME ENDED/ INITIALS

Source: North Carolina Baptist Hospital, Winston-Salem, NC

FIGURE
5

INSTABILITY CRITERIA

NORTH CAROLINA BAPTIST HOSPITAL

ADULT PHYSIOLOGIC INSTABILITY CRITERIA

(Trigger Tool – Adult)

*Patient assessment is essential to know individual baseline

RN is worried about the patient and/or patient meets any of the following:

Criteria	Low	High
Temp (oral)	<95°F	>102°F
(rectal)	<96°F	>103°F
Respiratory rate		>35 breaths/min for >30 min
O$_2$ Sat. (SpO$_2$)	<93% with supplemental O$_2$	
ABG	pH<7.25 pO$_2$<50 mm/Hg HCO3 <18	pCO2>60mm/Hg
Cardiac heart rate	<40 beats/min	>130 beats/min
Systolic BP	<85mmHg	>200mmHg
Level of consciousness	Acute change in mental status, agitation, restlessness, or acute decrease in GCS 2	

Source: North Carolina Baptist Hospital, Winston-Salem, NC

CASE STUDY — QUEEN'S MEDICAL CENTER, HONOLULU

Note: In this case study, author Della Lin details the development of the rapid response team initiative at her facility, Queen's Medical Center.

When the initial data from Rinaldo Bellomo's medical emergency team study on Australian METs was published in 2003, we shared the information with our Code 500 and ICU teams. The teams responded that there was already an effort underway to encourage nurses on the floors to call before the actual code. In addition, the Code 500 team was in the process of developing adult emergency protocols for symptoms such as chest pain and hypoglycemia.

Our multidisciplinary ICU special care committee and medical executive committee were in the process of approving these protocols for floor nurses to institute without a physician order.

Two key events

The idea lay dormant for a couple of years before two events occurred synergistically. In the first event, Queen's started a patient safety fellowship program in which each year, two or three individuals are selected from a pool of employee applicants to commit a portion of their time to a patient safety–focused program. These individuals dedicate three days per month actively engaged in patient safety efforts.

Managers support the program by allocating time commitment hours to the home cost center, and the vice president level of leadership endorses it as well. The fellows spend the year going through an experiential educational curriculum—including readings, serving on our patient safety committee, selecting a project area of interest that is presented as a poster at the hospital's annual statewide patient safety conference, and being involved with other subcommittees and activities generated through the patient safety committee. This grassroots education is meant to diffuse and integrate patient safety at the frontline level and give our patient safety committee additional perspective at the "sharp end."

In 2005, both fellows were nurses: Lois Han, RN, came from the surgical ICU, and Vanessa Lyons, RN, came from a general medical/surgical floor. The focus area of interest they chose was in communication and nursing satisfaction, but that interest it quickly grew to a distinct passion and interest in piloting rapid response teams (RRT).

The second event was that our 2005 safety conference was conducted in collaboration with the Institute for Health Care Improvement (IHI). IHI rolled out the 100,000 Lives campaign in December 2004, making our February 2005 conference an excellent backdrop for jump-starting hospital sites in Hawaii. Senior IHI Fellow Roger Resar, MD, provided compelling reasons to look at system redesign and prevent avoidable deaths. When our ICU team representative said the hospital was already doing so, Resar shot back, "Then don't be afraid to look at your data and see if it supports your conclusions."

Moving forward

With both a leadership and a grassroots push, the RRT initiative quickly moved forward. A review of our data found that although we had put systems and intended resources into place to improve the earlier rescue of patients, the resources were not being used: Only one of the previous 23 codes on the floor had used the adult emergency protocols. We now knew that we could do better.

The enthusiasm of the two patient safety fellows created a setting in which to pilot a new RRT that would operate alongside existing resource teams. One patient safety fellow became a nurse on the RRT, and the other offered her unit to test the initiative. Members of our RRT include an ICU-trained nurse, an ICU-trained respiratory therapist, and a pharmacist (the latter by phone consultation). The nurse manager selects team members not only for their clinical skills but also for their desire to teach and ability to communicate effectively under potentially challenging conditions.

The RRT is expected to be
- responsive—always go, no questions asked
- courteous
- willing to provide clinical expertise to the primary nurse assigned to the patient, not to take over the care of the patient
- supportive
- willing to teach and answer questions

Additionally, to clarify how this team was to operate alongside other emergency resource systems, we used a diagram to reflect early use of the rapid response team.

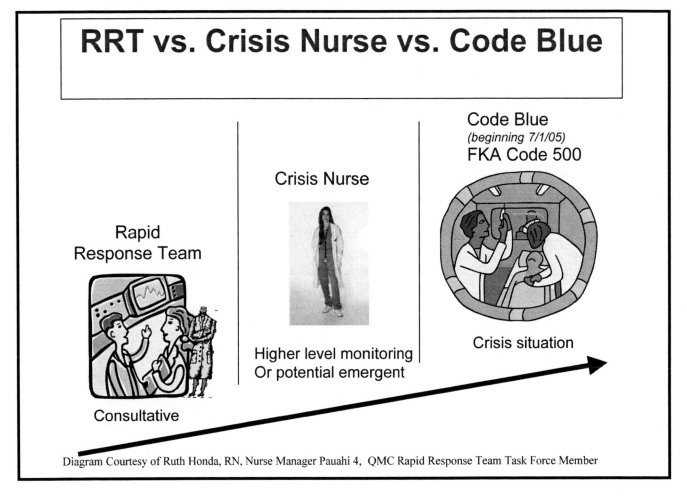

RRT vs. Crisis Nurse vs. Code Blue

Code Blue
(beginning 7/1/05)
FKA Code 500

Crisis Nurse

Rapid
Response Team

Crisis situation

Higher level monitoring
Or potential emergent

Consultative

Diagram Courtesy of Ruth Honda, RN, Nurse Manager Pauahi 4, QMC Rapid Response Team Task Force Member

Although the strategies have contributed to the overall measurement goal of reducing unplanned returns to the ICU, Brown says they also share a common focus: clearer communication.

Early win

One of the early pilot RRT calls received particular positive feedback from one of the hospital's vascular surgeons. The patient, who was on a medical/surgical floor, had a hospitalist for a primary attending. The consulting surgeon on the case was away for the weekend and had handed off care to a covering vascular surgeon colleague. The patient's primary care nurse became concerned with the patient's leg and called the weekend hospitalist. The hospitalist—with the telephone information received—did not feel that there was need for immediate intervention and asked that the patient be observed. The nurse, still having an uncomfortable "gut feeling," called the RRT. The RRT's assessment at the bedside included recommending that the patient be seen at the bedside by the surgeon. The surgeon found the patient's leg to be compromised by an evolving compartment syndrome. The patient required surgical intervention.

The early win in this case was that the new RRT system removed barriers that might have previously existed for the nurse to continue to communicate her concerns. By keeping channels open to escalate concerns, the patient was able to receive prompt and timely care.

Preparing to expand the program

Now that the program has expanded to a fourth unit, the number of calls has increased, and concerns about expansion are being deliberated. Because the current team consists of nurses and RTs with daily patient care assignments/responsibilities, the options are as follows:

1) Expand the teams to provide backup teams as necessary

2) Continue to limit the team membership and focus on expanding and ensuring backup of patient care responsibilities on the home unit

Either way, the initiative task force is intent on designing the expansion for success. Therefore, the task force is making sure that it reflects on evaluations from

- the RRTs themselves
- the pilot units
- the physicians whose patients were affected by the RRT intervention

In addition, the task force will review carefully the resources available, the lessons learned, and the opportunity for patient rescue within the context of this organization, before moving ahead on a hospitalwide RRT expansion.

FIGURE
6

RAPID RESPONSE TEAM CALL RECORD

RAPID RESPONSE TEAM CALL RECORD
permanent medical record form

Trial extension includes Pauahi 4,5,6,7, & QET 7E, 7DH | Version #8 6/20/05

Date: _____ Unit/room #: _____ Time called: _____ Time event ended: _____

Primary Reason for Call: *(NOTE: if your patient is unstable, please call crisis nurse instead)*

Staff Concerns	Change in vital signs	Change in LOC from baseline	Chest Pain	Fluid Status
X failure to respond to treatment or therapy X looks bad X unable to reach MD X something's wrong X I'm worried	≤ trending up or down in blood pressure and/or heart rate and/or respiratory rate that you are worried about	X drowsy X confused X agitated/restless X lethargic X unresponsive	X new X recurring	X UOP < 50 cc/4 hrs

Use SBAR as your guide

Situation: (baseline vitals) Temp: _____ BP: _____ P: _____ RR: _____ SpO2: _____ GCS: _____
_____
_____
_____

Background: _ Recent transfer from ICU/Tele _ Recent fall _ Received blood/blood products recently _ New ER admit ì Recent procedure done (Endo, Imaging, on unit, etc) * Recent medication effect, etc_____
_____
_____

Assessment: _____
_____
_____

Recommendations/Interventions:
_ Initiated Adult Emergency Protocols:
_____
_ Other actions taken: _____
_____

Patient Outcome
_ Stayed in room   _ Transfer to Tele   _ Transfer to ICU _ Other_____

NOTE: PLEASE CALL CRISIS NURSE IF YOU NEED HELP TRANSFERRING THE PT TO A HIGHER LEVEL OF CARE

R-R-T Responders: Name of RN: _____ Name of RCP: _____

Physician Notification: Date: _____ Time: _____
Name of Physician: _____   _ No, Reason: _____
                                              _ Yes, Reason: _____

Signature of Primary Nurse: _____ RN
PLEASE PLACE THIS FORM IN CHRONOLOGICAL ORDER IN THE PROGRESS NOTE SECTION OF THE MEDICAL RECORD

FIGURE 7

BASELINE REVIEW OF CODES OUTSIDE ICU

MR #_____   Code location _____

Patient (circle one)   Medical   Surgical

Did Patient Survive Code?   YES   NO
      If yes, days in ICU after code   _____
           days in hospital after code   _____

Hospital admission: Was the patient initially placed in an ICU?   YES   NO

          Was the patient hospitalized for comfort care only?   YES   NO

          New admission to unit within 24 hours? (circle)   ED   ICU   Other

24 hours before event:	YES	Comments
Hemodynamics		
Acute Change in SBP < 90		
MAP < 70 calc:[(SBP) +(DBPx2)] / 3		
MAP > 130		
HR < 45		
HR > 125		
Respiratory		
RR < 10		
RR > 28		
Change in O2 Sat < 90 with O2		
Level of Consciousness		
Altered mental status		
Agitation/restlessness		
Urine Output		
Change in UO to < 50ml in 4 hrs		
Pain		
Chest pain		
Gut feeling		
Documented worried about patient		
Called MD within 2/4/6 hours		
Called RT within 2/4/6 hours		
Called Crisis Nurse within 2/4/6		
Called ICU physician within 2/4/6		

Source: Queen's Medical Center, Honolulu. Reprinted with permission

FIGURE 8 — RAPID RESPONSE TEAM EVALUATION FORM

Date of Event: _____ Time of Event: _____ Place of Event *(Dept/Unit of Patient):* _____

Patient Name: _____ Medical Record #: _____ Acct #: _____
                                          (6 digit)   *(8 digit)*

Please answer the following questions with respect to the RRT Event.

The Primary Nurse of the patient should complete this form and return it within 24 hours

Please answer each question and mark your responses with an "X" when appropriate

#	Question	Disagree Strongly 1	Disagree Slightly 2	Neutral 3	Agree slightly 4	Agree Strongly 5
1	The RRT arrived in a timely manner					
2	The RRT **nurse** was knowledgeable and efficient in assessing and implementing care needs					
3	The RRT **respiratory care therapist** was knowledgeable and efficient in assessing and implementing care needs.					
4	Communication to and from the RRT **nurse and/or respiratory care therapist** was effective in facilitating the delivery of care.					
5	The RRT was courteous and helpful.					
6	Patient outcome was improved because of RRTassistance.					
7	I worked collaboratively with the RRT and the attending physician/resident.					
8	In working with the RRT I feel more comfortable and confident in managing patient in pre or potential crisis.					
9	The RRT helped me to learn something new or something I should have done.					
10	The RRT helped me to see or understand the "big picture" on managing the patient's care.					
11	EDUCATION: *(Briefly describe what you learned)*					
12	PROCESS IMPROVEMENT: *(Briefly describe a change in a patient care process that could help improve patient care)*					
13	ADDITIONAL COMMENTS:					

Primary Nurse (Print name)_____ (Signature) _____

Please return completed form to Nurse Manager, QET 4C within 24 hours of event.

Adapted from Missouri Baptist, Memphis by Queen's Medical Center. Reprinted by permission

QUEEN'S MEDICAL CENTER RRT
MEDICAL STAFF SURVEY

Recently, one of your patients was seen by the newly implemented Rapid Response Team. During the initial phases of this program roll-out, your opinion and feedback are critically important.

Thank you for taking the time to complete this survey. We have provided you with the patient's name and call date.

Patient's Name _____

Call Date _____

1. I was aware that a rapid response team was called to consult on my patient.   Y   N

If yes, please continue the survey (SA=Strongly agree, A=Agree, N=Neither agree nor disagree, D=Disagree, SD=Strongly disagree):

2. I received a call regarding the changing condition on my patient in a timely manner.

SA A N D SD

3. The RRT call potentially prevented a more serious clinical situation from occurring.

SA A N D SD

4. The RRT shed new light on the clinical situation.   SA A N D SD

5. The team provided coordination and communication which helped me manage my patient.

SA A N D SD

6. The team provided timely recommendations and interventions which helped in the management of my patient.

SA A N D SD

7. The team provided collaborative support to the primary nurse.   SA A N D SD

8. The rapid response team is a valuable new resource to this hospital.   SA A N D SD

Comments (please feel free to add any comments, suggestions):

Thank you for your time. We value your input and response.

Source: Queen's Medical Center, Honolulu.

CASE STUDY	SOUTHWESTERN VERMONT MEDICAL CENTER, BENNINGTON, VT

The value of having a rapid response team (RRT) is starting to sink in for the staff at Southwestern Vermont Health System. "People start realizing that this can really happen here," says **Avis Hayden, PhD, PT,** organizational development specialist in the patient/resident safety department at the 99-bed community hospital. The program's success is partly due to a leadership priority that "we are a learning organization."

Southwestern Vermont chose to create a team consisting of a hospitalist and respiratory therapist, opting not to include a nurse in their initial teams. "We have a small number of ICU nurses, and we wanted to make sure that we did not compromise care in those units," explains Hayden.

MEC involved in rapid response effort

The medical executive committee (MEC) played a vital role in the success of the RRT, staying involved and integrated in all quality initiatives implemented at the hospital. "The medical executive committee has formal planning every year and sets goals. They are willing to listen."

The facility also conducted education during the RRT roll-out and implementation, Hayden says.

In addition, Chief Medical Safety Officer **Robert Pezzulich, MD,** was previously the chief of staff at Southwestern Vermont. His leadership continues the important link between the operational initiatives and the medical staff leadership. "Our quest is to become as safe as possible," he adds.

Communication is a SNAP

At around the same time that the RRT initiative was being piloted, the organization began a hospitalwide effort to put in place more structured communication in the clinical settings. Southwestern Vermont developed mnemonic device, similar to the SBAR communication tool, called SNAP

(Summerize, Narrate, Analyze, Plan). To facilitate education of frontline staff, the hospital launched an online learning program to teach the SNAP model.

To link the SNAP initiative with the RRT initiative, the hospital created educational lessons based on its early RRT experiences. "It was important for us to use our own stuff," Hayden reflects. The lessons present a series of cases that describe a patient scenario. These cases help to teach the criteria/parameters defined as red flags for calling an RRT. At points during the exercise, the learner is asked to frame the situation or call the RRT using the SNAP model.

Hayden cautions that the education piece is not always simple. "It is hard for nurse directors to give up more hours," she says. But, she notes, "The nurses who experience it love it."

Hayden, who holds a doctorate in human and organization systems, credits the RRT program's success to a balance of visible leadership and framing the new system in the context of real cases. When implementing such a system redesign and change, Hayden advises other hospitals to seek as much administrative buy-in as possible.

FIGURE 9

SOUTHWESTERN VERMONT MEDICAL CENTER CASE STORY

Introduction: The following is a sample case story used by Southwestern Vermont Medical Center to educate staff about the rapid response team initiative. The story is used with permission.

Mrs. N., a 74-year-old female, was admitted to the hospital following a heart attack. She is in Room 7. Mrs. N's regular doctor, Dr. Green, has turned over her after-hours care to the hospitalist, Dr. Connors.

On the shift report for the second day of Mrs. N's hospital stay, the nurses indicated that she was recovering nicely. Indeed, all morning she ran a heart rate between 90 and 100, her respiratory rate was 20, and her O2 saturation was 90 on room air. She has a good appetite. She voided 125 ml urine this morning. A physical therapist came to get Mrs. N. out of bed, and Mrs. N sat in a chair for more than an hour.

Her family has been here most of the day. Most of the time, she has between one and three visitors, which makes it difficult for her to rest.

SOUTHWESTERN VERMONT MEDICAL CENTER CASE STORY

As the afternoon progresses, she complains of being short of breath. Her breath sounds seem diminished. Her respiratory rate holds steady at 20. There is no current chest x-ray report in the chart.

At 1900, you walk into her room. She is clearly in respiratory distress. She has shallow respirations, complains of pain along the right side of her rib cage when she coughs, and has lung crackles with wheezes two-thirds of the way up. You suspect fluid in the lungs due to poor functioning of the heart muscle, a common complication of heart attack.

You are worried about these symptoms. You place a rapid response call. How do you organize your thoughts? Use SNAP algorithm.

Follow-up

The rapid response team arrives. The team does not know the patient, but it has been advised by the nurse making the call that the symptoms appear to be consistent with fluid on the lungs due to poor heart function.

The hospitalist on the team checks vital signs, lab, and medical history, and he orders a chest x-ray. He suspects that the respiratory distress is not due to fluid in the lungs but to spasm of bronchioles due to chronic lung disease. He administers medication by nebulizer and anti-inflammatory meds by IV. Patient improves dramatically over the next two hours.

Although the nurse's rapid response call seemed related to heart symptoms, what mattered most was that the nurse noted the symptoms and made the call.

FIGURE 10

SNAP CALL SCRIPT

Report to Hospitalist or Rapid Response Team about a critical situation

S	<u>Summarize:</u> **State your name, unit:** **I am calling about** <u>\<patient name, location, and **brief** summary of situation\></u>. **The patient's code status is** <u>\<code status\></u> **The patient's vital signs are:** **Pressure: _____** **Pulse: _____** over 200 systolic over 130 less than 90 systolic less than 40 30 mmHg below usual **Respiration: _____** **Temperature: _____** less than 8 less than 96 over 24 over 104
N	<u>Narrate:</u> **The patient's pertinent medical history is:** **The patient's mental status is:** 　　Alert and oriented to person place and time. 　　Confused and cooperative or non-cooperative 　　Delirious 　　Agitated or combative 　　Lethargic but conversant and able to swallow 　　Stuporous and not talking clearly and possibly not able to swallow 　　Comatose. Eyes closed. Not responding to stimulation. **The patient is not or is on oxygen.** 　　The patient has been on _____ (l/min) or (%) oxygen for _____ minutes (hours) 　　The oximeter is reading _____% 　　The oximeter does not detect a good pulse and is giving erratic readings. **Brief synopsis of recent interventions:**
A	<u>Analyze:</u> 　　**This is what I think the problem is:** <u>\<say what you think is the problem\></u> 　　**The problem seems to be cardiac infection neurologic respiratory _____** 　　**I am afraid the patient is going to arrest.** 　　**I am not sure what the problem is but the patient is deteriorating.** 　　**The patient seems to be unstable and may get worse, we need to do something.**
P	<u>Propose Action:</u> **I suggest or request that you** <u>\<say what you would like to see done\></u>. 　　transfer the patient to critical care 　　come to see the patient at this time. 　　Talk to the patient or family about code status. 　　Contact Rapid Response Team member 　　Ask for a consultant to see the patient now. **Are any tests needed:** 　　Do you need any tests like CXR, ABG, EKG, CBC, or BMP? 　　Others? **If a change in treatment is ordered then ask:** 　　How often do you want vital signs? 　　How long to you expect this problem will last? 　　If the patient does not get better when would you want us to call again?

Source: Adapted from Michael Leonard, MD, for Southwestern Vermont Hospital. Reprinted with permission.